JUST SMILE

Abby Hegewald

Formatting by Pink Umbrella Books

Edited by Autumn McAlpin, Adrienne Quintana, and Marnae Kelley

Cover Design by Olivia Johnston

For Josh, Sophie, Ben & Sam
the four people who continue to make me smile

Preface.

After surviving the first year on my own without Kevin, I started writing our story. Three years later I had a completed manuscript that my dear friend and published author Autumn McAlpin had red lined three times for me that I no longer had intentions of publishing. Writing it had served its purpose: it had given *me* purpose as I examined my life and found meaning. In 2021, the ten year mark of Kevin's passing, I decided to print the book for my children. Fortune and fate stepped in when an extra copy landed on the desk of the talented Adrienne Quintana, thanks to Kelly Moody, who continues to have a hand in my life. I am grateful for my children's support in publishing this book. They loved it, and more importantly, they still love me. When I think of them, I use my real smile.

Table of Contents

Smile.

Every morning before I walk out the door, the last thing I do is put on my smile. I smile as I parade my children up the hill to their school while still wearing my pajamas. I smile at children and neighbors and the hundreds of cars that drive past. I continue to smile throughout my entire day. I smile as I walk the aisles of the grocery store. I smile at the bank teller, the soccer coach, the piano teacher, the mailman. I smile and I smile and I smile. I have smiled all of my life and have forty-three years of creases to prove it. But those who don't know me have no idea how much effort it has taken to paste that smile on my face since September 20, 2011. Those who do know me look at me with either sympathy, pity, or a little curiosity. Some turn away; the brave ones smile back.

I learned the magic of a smile at a very young age. I have vivid memories of watching my mother do her hair and make-up in front of the mirror. Sitting on the floor with my legs crisscrossed outside the bathroom door, I would watch intently as she applied her Avon cosmetics, the finale a thick coat of bright red lipstick. She then turned her attention to her platinum blonde hair, which she would aggressively back comb and tease into an intricate nest. After a few finishing touches and a solid spray of Aqua Net, she would look at herself in the mirror—and smile. And at that moment, I witnessed the most amazing thing: my mother dazzled. Despite her allegiance to the ritual, it wasn't the platinum perch or ruby red lips, but the smile that made her beautiful.

When I met Kevin Hegewald, I remember thinking I had never seen such a big smile. Well, that's not really true. I actually remember thinking I had never seen such a big mouth. But then, he smiled. And that big mouth, just like my mom's big hair, suddenly became radiant. I was mesmerized, and I knew immediately that choosing to spend my life with Kevin would afford me years of reasons to smile back. With my blinders on, I failed to recognize that the man behind that dynamic smile was also capable of giving me plenty not to smile about, too. But never could I have imagined that one day he would leave me. And he would not only take with him that gigantic smile, but alter my ability to smile—and actually mean it—as well.

Born to Gab.

When I was born, the only thing big about me was my personality. Well, and my nose and my teeth, but they didn't fully manifest until much later. When my body stayed petite, my nose kept growing, as if to salute the gigantic permanent teeth coming in below. Fortunately, fate stepped in and took care of both problems. Breaking my nose in a car accident my senior year in high school provided the opportunity to restore it to a more proportionate size, and extracting four permanent front teeth softened the appearance of my overcrowded mouth. My dentist is possibly the only person in the world who ever said I had a small mouth. Everybody else who knew me as a child testified to a different truth: I loved to talk.

Abigail no-middle-name Cannon. Born on the sixth of July, my mom called me a left-over firecracker. Like a firecracker, I made a lot of loud noise. Fortunately, I was given an older sister who was born with a gift to listen. From our appearances, Kim and I looked like opposites. Her thick, long brown hair and tall, healthy build stood in stark contrast to my wispy blonde hair and pint-sized physique. But none of my siblings looked like one another. When my mom chose her babies in heaven, she must have likened it to a stop inside a See's candy store and ordered one of each—five babies each with a distinct hair color: dark brown, blonde, red, jet black, and auburn. As the designated blonde in the family, I lived my life trying to prove that blondes have more fun. My "fun" personality led me to a career of scrubbing gum off the bottom of classroom desks, while Kim's sophistication earned her a seat at a corporate desk and a framed MBA. But, despite our differences, we were a perfect match: I would talk, and Kim would listen.

One summer when we traveled to North Carolina to visit my mom's relatives, my dad was left behind with the project to paint my bedroom. I knew exactly what color I wanted it to be: pink. I still remember my mom's facial contortion when we returned home to discover that my dad had chosen to paint with Pepto Bismol. The color was bold. It was bright. It was nauseating. It was perfect. But the feature I loved the most about my bedroom was the cut-out window that connected to Kim's bedroom. We spent countless hours transforming the opening into a library book check-out station, a post office window, or a fast-food drive through. But the best part of sharing a window was when night came, and I could continue to talk to Kim while we were snuggled in our own beds. I would carry on a spirited one-sided conversation until I eventually noticed the silence from the other room. I would reluctantly ask, "Kim, are you asleep?" And when she would respond "yes," I would believe her, and close my eyes and fall asleep.

Not everyone tolerated my voice box and the nonstop noise that protruded from it. Maybe because it wasn't just the talking, it was the volume and the incessant giggling that accompanied it. My younger brother Quen wrote me a letter posed from the *Guinness Book of World Records*. It congratulated me on breaking the world's record for loudest voice because they could hear me loud and clear in New York all the way from Utah. I felt honored.

My only memories of getting in trouble at school involve giggling at inopportune times. In my defense, it's hard to control the timing of loud outbursts when they're part of your innate nature. I would be sent out of the classroom to get control of myself but that was like sending an alcoholic to the liquor store. Out in the empty hall, I could let the uncontrollable laughter roll down the school corridor.

There was one class, however, where I made a concerted effort never to be ejected: Mr. Dean's. "Mean Dean"—the meanest U.S. History teacher in the history of the U.S. He looked as calm and cool as Magnum, P.I. He even sported a sexy brown mustache. But beneath his cool demeanor was a sadistic desire to torture children with long, boring lectures. Any student caught not paying attention would be invited to accompany him into the hall. The loud crash of a body coming into contact with metal lockers not only earned Mean Dean his nickname, but effectively disciplined and terrified an entire class.

Imagine my horror one morning when Mean Dean grumbled, "Cannon! Come up here." As the Hillside Jr. High Historian, one of my responsibilities was to occasionally deliver the morning announcements over the loudspeaker. Apparently, that morning the microphone amplified my already loud voice and, unbeknownst to me, a collective gasp and covering of the ears had occurred schoolwide. Mean Dean directed me to stand right up close on the other side of his desk. His words were slow and deliberate: "Hold the microphone SIX inches away from your mouth." Terrified, I did what came naturally—I giggled and then walked back to my seat, relieved that I had suffered only a reality check rather than a slam against the lockers.

I pretty much giggled and smiled my way through childhood. I didn't have any reason not to. Which means my life story won't ever be on Oprah's list because the only abuse my parents were guilty of was overpraising. My dad must have read the book, *How To Convince Your Children They Are Greater Than They Really Are*, and then spent so much time boosting our self-esteem he never got to the final chapter that included the fine print warnings about overdoing it. Surely he would have read about that one little consequence that might occur when a particular fabulous child spends her adult life wondering why her spouse doesn't think she's a fraction as wonderful as she thinks she is.

My Big Dreams.

1. Marry Brook Staples.
2. Become Olivia Newton-John.
3. Be a cheerleader.
4. Become a school teacher.
5. Be a mom of twelve kids.

Abigail Cannon, age 10.

I take full blame for the fact that I didn't marry Brook Staples. Dreamy Brook Staples, with his blonde hair and freckled face. Brook was my secret crush for six years after we bonded over *Sesame Street* and peanut butter and jelly sandwiches in kindergarten. And then I decided to run for sixth grade elementary school president … against Brook Staples. I must have wanted power more than love. Or thought I could have both. I beat him. And then he moved away the next year. So in hindsight, I guess I did the right thing.

I had another love affair that began in the fifth grade: Olivia Newton-John. My parents took us to see the movie *Grease*, and I was a goner. I spent the next year of my life belting out "Hopelessly Devoted" alongside my 8-track *Grease* soundtrack, practicing my Australian accent, and wearing my hair slicked back in a high ponytail. I alternated between imitating the squeaky-clean Sandra Dee, and the totally hot, black-leather-clad, good-girl-gone-bad Sandy. Nothing was more fun than pretending to drop a cigarette and snuffing it out with my shoe while saying, "Tell me about it, stud," in my most sultry voice. I knew I was impersonating something I was not; I was definitely "won't go to bed 'til I'm legally wed" Sandra Dee material. But I also knew that my dream of actually *becoming* Olivia Newton-John was not really plausible either. (It was not until I watched *Grease* with Kevin when we were married that I was made aware of the sexually insinuating dialogue and lyrics. I thought "we got friendly down in the sa-a-a-nd" meant they built a sand castle together. I am grateful to know that my mom and I shared the same naiveté.)

With the Marry Brook Staples and Become Olivia Newton-John dreams out of the way, I now could focus on the one dream that I was born to achieve: be a cheerleader. I had three strong advantages:

1. Obviously my loud and enthusiastic voice.

2. I come from cheerleader genes. My mom was a high school varsity cheerleader for the Elizabeth City High Yellow Jackets. Senior class population: 94. She was cute, blonde, and could yell, three traits I happened to inherit.

3. I was blessed with long, pencil-thin legs attached to my armpits. Unfortunately, those same legs were as limber as a wooden pencil.

Unlike today, where you can choose cheerleading as your career when you are three years old, there were not many opportunities to achieve my dream. In fact, there were no sports teams to cheer for at Hillside Jr. High. So once a year the faculty would put together a single basketball game—The Bombers vs. The Rockets—with cheerleaders! An unfortunate series of events occurred: I had an ear infection, which led to a penicillin prescription, which uncovered a newly discovered allergic reaction, which caused me to be covered from head-to-toe with a rash of red dots … on the day of cheerleader tryouts. But I was not to be deterred from my destiny. After spending the school day in bed, I got up and pulled on a pair of red shorts and a red-and-white striped t-shirt to wear to the after-school tryouts. I have no idea if I was trying to disguise or match the red bumps covering my body. I obviously didn't think it was that big of a deal … until I took center stage and saw the horrified, jaw-dropped reaction of the judges. At that moment I remember thinking, "Just smile. Act like nothing is wrong." I was mentally willing the judges to be drawn to my dynamic smile rather than my grotesquely polka-dot-infested body. Whether this worked or not, the judges were not distracted enough to notice my inability to kick higher than three inches. I went home, crawled back into bed, and didn't even bother showing up the next day to see the posted list of lucky girls who would be instantly catapulted to popular status.

I had to wait four more years for my next opportunity, this time the big leagues—high school. An advantage of trying out for cheerleader at Highland High School was the cheerleaders were not expected to do any fancy gymnastic tricks; cartwheels were admired. (Although I never could get my legs to go over my head.) It was more important to be cute and peppy and light enough that the boy cheerleaders with no muscles could still lift you. That was me! I was cute and peppy; my dad told me that all of the time. Unfortunately, I lost to girls that were much cuter and peppier and probably were told that by people other than their dads. One more dream dashed. Time to focus on the attainable.

I loved everything about the thought of being a school teacher. I am one of those people that inhale when opening a new box of crayons. School supply shopping—thrilling. Desks organized in straight rows—exhilarating. The power a teacher has—intoxicating. I was destined to be the one in charge; to have full control over who gets to talk when, who gets to use the restroom pass, and who gets to stand at the front of the line. My school teaching dream was to follow in my mom's footsteps: she taught high school English for one year before quitting to have a baby. That's exactly the plan I intended to follow. Sure, I wanted to gain all of that knowledge and power to help other children, but I also wanted to use it on my own. As I saw it, being a mom was the ideal job because I could still command the respect and power that comes from being a teacher but from the comfort of my own home. So as much as I wanted to be a school teacher, my ultimate dream was to be a mom.

I spent my entire childhood jumping from learning one skill to the next. I danced—ballet, tap, jazz. I learned sports—tennis, swimming, skiing. I played instruments—piano, violin, voice. And what do I have to show for it all? I am a very well-rounded person who can do a lot of things mediocrely. But I didn't care that I never excelled at anything. I believed that when I became a mom I would finally be extraordinary at something—like a prodigy mom. And I was planning on having TWELVE children. I have Frank Gilbreth to thank for wanting twelve kids. One summer my mom read *Cheaper by the Dozen* to me and my siblings. I was far too naive to know that the title was false advertising and didn't apply to children. And I was convinced that if I had twelve kids I would never be lonely.

In the pursuit of my dreams, two significant events happened the year I graduated from college: I began teaching school and experienced what I thought would be the hardest year of my life. And, I met Kevin Hegewald, who introduced me to a whole new definition of the word *hard*.

Prepared for Hard Things.

When I graduated from the University of Utah in elementary education, I was twenty-two years old, overly optimistic, untainted by the real world, and eager to save mankind one child at a time. I never wavered from wanting to become a school teacher. Until I actually became one.

I was hired in October 1990 to teach fifth grade at Bennion Elementary School, an inner-city school in Salt Lake City. I was told the deciding factor in being chosen was my impeccable handwriting, which looks much like the Comic New Sans font. All of those years of writing "Miss Cannon" with perfectly shaped letters all over the covers of my notebooks paid off!

I was assigned a class of thirty-eight fifth graders. The year-round school started in July and by the time I was hired in October, I was the third teacher assigned to this class. (First red flag.) The location of my classroom proved to be a huge disadvantage. We met in the music room, the only upper-grade classroom on the first floor, and were tucked away in the corner of the school. I was completely isolated and insulated from someone else hearing me scream for help. (Second red flag.) The only bonus of the music room was it was furnished with a piano. However, the only playing it ever received was when a student ran across the keys trying to escape.

The track record of this class scared me. My classroom scared me. But nothing scared me more than Billy Bates. This was the kid nobody else wanted. Little did I know that more than half of my class list fit this criteria. But everybody had warned me about Billy Bates: the teachers, the custodian, even the lunch ladies. My nightmares starred Billy Bates, turning me so *Psycho*, I was convinced his name was actually Norman. Facing my fears, I called Billy on the phone, introduced myself, and asked him if he would please come help me set up my classroom. He accepted.

When Billy walked in, I had a hard time imagining that this good-looking, blonde-haired and blue-eyed kid could be the nightmare everyone was describing. I put Billy to work arranging the desks and quickly learned which students needed to be near the front, which ones couldn't sit by each other, and which ones Billy strongly disliked. Billy chose a seat on the front row, strategically placed next to the door for a quick getaway. I struck a deal with the purported devil that day. When he told me how much he liked to read, I told him as long as he completed his assignments, he could read all day long for as long as he would like.

Eleven weeks. That's how long I lasted before I had my resignation speech rehearsed in my head to deliver to the principal. I was just hanging on until Christmas break. I had spent the past eleven weeks crying myself to sleep every night. Four years at an accredited university did not prepare me for how to handle this class and all of its issues. I had been handed fifth-grade books and curriculum and goals that needed to be met and a class full of children that had bigger issues to deal with than learning the state capital of Oklahoma. (Which by the way, is the easiest one because it is Oklahoma City.) My paradigm of the world was abruptly shifting as I was exposed to the social problems of homelessness, child abuse, gang activity, foster care, sexual promiscuity, and, quite honestly, my heart couldn't take it any more. I'd witnessed too many depressing and disturbing situations. I was traumatized watching Margaret flinch every time her dad raised his hand. Or seeing Craig being ostracized because of the stench of his unwashed clothes. Or when Roberto, after breaking my classroom window with a rock, was hauled off by his grandma—the only person available because his dad was in prison for stabbing his mom. I was proud that I had lasted as long as eleven weeks. Prior, two teachers had come and gone in that time; I could quit with my head held high.

The much anticipated and prayed for moment finally arrived. As soon as the dismissal bell rang on Friday before the two week Christmas break, I walked into the principal's office. My goal was to get in and out as quickly as possible, hopefully with a tiny bit of self-respect still intact. I needed to be professional. Brief. To the point. Unemotional.

"Mr. García, I'd like to talk to you about my class … I'm sorry I won't be able to continue teaching."

"What seems to be the problem?" he responded as he directed me to a chair.

"Well, it's just that I wasn't prepared to deal with such difficult and disrespectful students who come from such broken homes and dysfunctional families that they already behave like juvenile delinquents knocking over desks and throwing punches and hurling foul words at me like stones thrown at an adulteress and honestly I want to throw up every Sunday night at just the thought of having to face my class the next morning" … is what I wanted to say. But …

"I've just had a very difficult time with my students" … is what I actually said, with my body shaking as much as my voice.

"Miss Cannon. We didn't hire you because of your impeccable handwriting. Although it didn't hurt. But we hired you because you are capable."

I spent two hours in the principal's office coming up with strategies for how I could feel more supported and especially trying to believe this man who thought I was capable. So I spent my Christmas break personally visiting each one of my thirty-eight students. Looking back on it, it probably wasn't the wisest thing to do, traipsing from apartment to apartment, with half of them displaying "Beware of Dog" or "NO Visitors Welcome" signs hanging from their chain-link gates. I was greeted by suspicious parents and curious students, and if they happened to invite me in, I would take a few minutes and sit on the couch while they stared at me before leaving a small gift and searching for the next unsuspecting student's house.

I returned to my class in January. I never told anyone at school about my Christmas adventure, but one day it all came out.

With no surrounding classrooms to lend aid, I was unable to physically escort a disruptive student to the office. I was also smart enough to know that they wouldn't make it there on their own. (Okay, well, I learned that lesson after a student of mine was reported missing.) My best strategy was total lock-down in my classroom. All back-talking, name-calling, pushing, teasing, or poking, I dealt with on my own. But two things resulted in an immediate trip to the principal's office: swearing or vulgar language and punching another student. One day, Isaac broke both rules.

Isaac was escorted to the office, his parents were called, and for some reason, this time, they actually came. Details were disclosed how I had visited their home during Christmas, and Isaac's parents were not going to allow their son to make my life difficult. Mr. García met me in my classroom at the end of the day. With a skeptical look, he asked, "Did you visit Isaac over Christmas break?"

"Yes."

"Did you visit all of your students?"

"Yes."

He just shook his head. It was kind of a "you are a stupid girl" head shake, and a "there must be a district policy about this" head shake, but a little bit of a "I knew there was more to you than just your pretty handwriting" in there, too.

I survived. One day at a time. I learned to love the weekends, and hate Sunday nights. Sadly, I can say I doubt any of my students learned anything that year. Well, I should say, learned anything from the fifth-grade curriculum. My classroom was chaos and I was in survival mode. Hopefully they all learned that hitting and punching and spitting and name calling don't get you anywhere except the principal's office.

Surprisingly, I returned the next year. They moved me upstairs with the other upper-grade classrooms. So now when I screamed for help, someone always came running. The three years I taught at Bennion Elementary School changed me. I shed my innocence, but I learned that I am a strong person and I can handle hard things. And I learned that hard things are a lot easier to handle if you have someone who will come running to your rescue.

My Voice.

Kevin said he fell in love with me before he even saw me. We were both students at the University of Utah. I was diligently pursuing my elementary education dream, and I belonged to a Greek sorority on the side. Kevin was a pre-med student, belonged to a Greek fraternity, played in a rock band, and worked two other jobs. Kevin claimed he was standing outside of the Sigma Chi house when he heard me, and he instantly knew he wanted to meet the girl with that laugh. He was patient. A year later, I had graduated and was barely surviving teaching, when we were lined up by our best friends—Darin, Kevin's childhood friend, business associate, and partner in crime; and Susie, Darin's fiancée, my friend, and the best thing that came out of joining Chi Omega. It could have been considered a blind date, but once Kevin and I met, I instantly recognized his face, and he instantly recognized my voice.

Kevin picked me up in his faded jeans and green-and-white rugby shirt, with his blonde hair swooping over his enormous round glasses, and we drove two hours with Darin and Susie to Wendover, Utah. Let me clarify—West Wendover, Nevada. Home to 1,632. Google "what to do in Wendover" and you'll be rewarded with results such as, "The Rainbow Hotel has a swimming pool and fitness room" or "During the summer, baseball teams play on the ball diamond behind the Rainbow" or "Check out the shopping center along with the liquor store on the outskirts of town past the Rainbow Hotel." That's because the only reason anyone would stop in Wendover is to visit the casino, conveniently located inside … the Rainbow Hotel.

A two hour drive afforded a lot of time to get to know each other, and my gift of gab was definitely matched, if not surpassed.

He told me all about his family. He was the middle child, with two older brothers and a younger brother and sister. His parents, Rudi and Eva Hegewald, both escaped from East Germany—his dad by jumping from a moving train, and his mom by obtaining a permit to visit a "sick aunt" who didn't exist. They immigrated to Salt Lake City in 1957 and bought a piece of land. Kevin lived in a house his dad built with a view of Mount Olympus in the backyard.

"Every family photo we've ever taken has the mountain as the backdrop," he told me. "I'm glad my house is across the lane from the elementary school because one time I threw a banana across the lunch tables and accidentally broke a window. It made for a quick getaway." He laughed.

"Of course I really got in trouble when we were on our one and only family trip to California and I did a huge cannonball off the diving board and landed on top of my Tante Anita's head. Right after she had ear surgery."

"At least the police weren't called," Darin interjected.

The police didn't get involved until his high school years when he streaked past Denny's restaurant wearing only his underwear, or later, when he stole a truckload of trout from a state fish hatchery. Darin was more than happy to help provide the dirty details.

I also learned all about his jobs. As a child, in the summers he pulled weeds, in the winters he shoveled snow, and in all seasons, he delivered newspapers. Presently, he was working three jobs. He played the electric guitar in a band called Probable Cause, and even though he got paid, he would have played for free. He worked as a phlebotomist, traveling to house-bound patients to draw their blood, and had his sights on becoming a medical doctor. His final job, responsible for his dirty fingernails, was Mobilube—a business he started with Darin, changing oil in people's cars at their home or work location.

I was fascinated by Kevin's unique upbringing, in awe of his work ethic, and a little apprehensive because of his exploits. But then came the subject of animals. Kevin loved all animals. Except dogs. I think having a newspaper route eliminated that love affair. He had raised chickens and bunnies and used his birthday money one year to buy a pet cockatiel he named Henry. But Kevin's fondest devotion was to his pigeons. He described in detail his attempts at raising a flock of pigeons—emphasis on the word *attempt*. I heard about pigeons being taken out by hawks and by a mean neighbor's bb gun, by his carelessness of leaving the cage open, and by their inability to make it home after being released 400 miles away in Lake Powell. On and on and on. Had I known of Kevin's particular obsession with the animal kingdom, I might not have accepted his invitation for a date. Of course, had he known what an animal-hater I am, he might not have asked me.

I spent the night inhaling second-hand smoke with Susie, while we watched Kevin and Darin attempt to play cards. I felt like a James Bond girl watching over Kevin's shoulder, except instead of being surrounded by supermodels in cufflinks and sequins, we were surrounded by homeless-looking people wearing Hawaiian shirts and socks with flip-flops. After Kevin had lost his allocated gambling funds, he tried his luck on the dance floor. His dance skills demonstrated that he was much more comfortable playing the electric guitar while other people danced.

But when a slow song came on, he pulled me close and said, "I love the smell of Liz Claiborne."

I found him intriguing, especially as he could distinguish my perfume over the smoke and sweat smell that I was reeking of.

The next day, I reportedly told my mom that despite the date being fun, a future with Kevin Hegewald was not an option because:

1. He wanted to be a doctor (of humans, not animals). And yes, he might be able to afford my dream family of eight children—I had reasonably lowered it from twelve—but he wouldn't be around to help me raise them. And …

2. I would spend the rest of my life having to slowly spell out my last name.

Kevin always proudly reported that he never dated another person after our first date. I can't say the same. But ten months later, we were engaged to be married, and at each one of my bridal showers, I was forced to divulge the details of our first date to grungy Wendover. Lesson to be learned: if you grow up in a predominantly Mormon community that shuns gambling and smoking, save going to a casino for the second date.

Kevin and I were a classic case of opposites attract. I've never truly understood the ideology behind that. I suppose, idealistically, the two people complete each other because they each bring a whole bag of stuff that the other doesn't have. But what if you don't want what's in their bag?

Kevin's bag was filled with dreams of a life of adventure. He wanted to scale mountains, explore jungles, live in Alaska, become a doctor and save lives. I just wanted to be a mom, and not in Alaska. But something had sparked between us, so I pretended to like camping and adventure, and Kevin pretended to want eight children. And right there is the foundation of the next 1,000 arguments of our married life. Of course, Kevin seemed to get past the disappointment of me not accompanying him on his expeditions much faster than I got past my resentment that he would leave to go on them.

On June 23, 1992, we committed to love one another for better or worse, for richer or poorer, in sickness or in health. We had hoped there would be more better, richer, and health.

Ocean Girl.

During our first year of marriage, Kevin was accepted to Eastern Virginia Medical School in Norfolk. That's pronounced "Nawfuk" to real Southerners like myself. Sure, growing up, my body resided in Salt Lake City, Utah, but my soul lived on the sandy white beaches of the Outer Banks of North Carolina. I was thrilled at the prospect of introducing Kevin to a piece of my childhood, and I was equally excited to use the Southern drawl I had perfected in my youth.

At a young age, I must have swallowed enough salt water to permanently alter my veins because I am definitely happiest when I am near the ocean. Note the word near. I don't need to be *in* the ocean, just close enough to be able to breathe it in.

I attribute my love for the ocean to my mother. (See, Mom, I have now given you credit for one more thing besides my blonde hair, ability to yell, and misguided perceptions that teaching school and having twelve children are good ideas.)

My mother grew up in Elizabeth City, North Carolina. The only thing "city" about Elizabeth City was the one traffic light running through the middle of the town. Her family owned a beautiful—in a weathered-wood, rustic kind of way—beach house in Nags Head, with enough rooms to sit and sleep a small army. I loved when my mom would tell us stories of her childhood at the beach. Looking as far as possible in both directions and not seeing another soul. Having to cross a mile of hot sand before reaching the ocean waves. Glass bottles of cold Pepsi-Cola drinks being delivered weekly to their cottage door. My favorite story involved my grandmother tying a rope around the waists of her seven children—the length of their rope determined by their age. Then my grandmother would sit on the beach with a large stake in the sand, the seven ropes tethered to it, with her children dangling on the other ends in the ocean. The ropes proved detrimental if a large wave was approaching and they were unable to swim out farther to avoid being pummeled. But even worse was when the kids were caught being unkind to one another, forcing my grandmother—at the end of her rope—to simply find the perpetrators' ropes and haul them in.

During my childhood, three weeks were reserved every other summer to fly from Utah back East. We'd spend the first few days with relatives in Elizabeth City, acclimating to the humidity and the foreign language spoken in the South. We loved to play in Grandma's attic—which was filled with costumes and smelled like mothballs—and Granddaddy's tire store—where he allowed us to climb up the high stacks of tires and jump down through the middle for an impressive game of hide-and-go-seek. The tires would turn our clothes and skin black, but we were occupied for hours searching for each other.

Usually after attending the Sunday church service, where my mom was treated like a celebrity after making a guest appearance on the organ, we would leave for the beach in a station wagon packed with towels, bedding, and coolers of food. Along the way, we'd sing songs through the great dismal swamp. Once we'd crossed the mile-long bridge, the luxuries of television and air conditioning were left behind as we entered a world of porch hammocks, beach grass, and sticky sheets.

Time miraculously stopped when we were at the beach house. The days melted into one another. The only distinguishing difference from one to the next—the calm or the storm of the ocean waves. Or the different sea creature sightings that would prevent us from entering the water. The story of my granddaddy out-swimming a shark inspired the habit of always being on the lookout for a black fin while lazily floating on an inner tube.

We did leave the beach for a few traditional outings. We would climb and run down the hot sand dunes of Jockey's Ridge. Visit Orvil and Wilbur Wright's Memorial and pace the lengths of their different flights. Spend an hour choosing a special Christmas ornament from the Christmas Shop and another hour choosing the perfect souvenir from Newman's Shell Shop.

When my feet were on the beaches of North Carolina, I felt complete. Like a sandy-blonde puzzle piece that fit perfectly into place. I loved cooking my Utah-white skin to a deep bronze, and spending every daylight hour reading books on the beach. Here was my perfect world. And now I could share it with Kevin.

To celebrate Kevin's medical school acceptance, and anticipating that I would need to find a new teaching job, I immediately went out and bought an entire wardrobe consisting of black and brown pants and tweed suit jackets with shoulder pads. This was my perception of the way Easterners dressed to teach school. We moved into the third floor of an apartment in what could be considered a posh area of Norfolk, directly across from Norfolk General Hospital—a structure that kind of contradicts what I just said about being in a posh area. I landed a dream job teaching second grade at The Williams School, the most charming private school, established inside an old colonial-style home. I'm almost certain this time it was my stylish new Eastern wardrobe that earned me the position. I'm sure I made quite the impression on the headmaster as a substitute teacher when I wore two mismatched shoes—both leather flats, one red, one brown—and acted with the confidence that I had done it on purpose. In reality, Kevin was asleep when I needed to leave so I had snuck into my closet and grabbed two shoes in the dark. I didn't notice until a student said something around 10:30 a.m. I couldn't believe how polite these privileged, Southern, private-school students were to keep that juicy tidbit to themselves all morning.

The downsides of living in Norfolk (other than the obscene way it is pronounced) were the year-round humidity, which made you moist and shiny all day, and the constant noise of sirens and trains. But the upside of living in Norfolk was my grandma lived only an hour away. Oh, how Kevin and I would anticipate the weekends we could escape to my grandmother's. When we arrived, we'd first visit with her in a sitting room in the back of the house. It was the most comfortable space, with a view of the gigantic magnolia trees, grapevine trellis, and child-sized doll house in her backyard. We'd hear about her health, and her neighbors' health, and the details of her week. My grandma's social calendar consisted of three events: church activities, doctor's appointments, and funerals. She would take a homemade cake or fresh baked loaf of bread to each of the above-listed functions. After an hour of visiting, she'd finally say, "Are y'all hungry?" and her kitchen table would soon be covered with a Southern spread of homemade fried chicken, Virginia ham, potato salad, pasta salad, fruit salad, and always at least three fresh homemade desserts. I'd argue that my grandmother was the best cook in all of North Carolina, and she had the physique to prove it. As starving medical students, we tried our best to come up for air between each delectable bite. Finally when our plates were scraped clean, we would ask Grandma if she needed help with anything. The answer almost always ended with a job for Kevin that required a power trimmer and a ladder.

My grandmother was there to hold our first two babies. I had continued to teach my second-grade class up to a week past Joshua's due date. I finally announced that I would not be returning, with or without a baby. When Joshua finally decided to enter the world, the nurses made a huge fuss over his blonde hair, an uncommon sight among the predominantly black-haired Norfolk General Hospital babies. But no one made a bigger fuss over him than I did. My dream of becoming a mother was finally fulfilled.

Having spent over twenty-four hours laboring in the hospital with Joshua, the second time around, I thought I would persevere for as long as possible at home. So while Kevin, my mom, and Joshua were enjoying peaceful dreams, I was enduring contractions in the bathroom by biting the towel rack. My naive game plan eventually led to me being wheeled into the hospital, fully dilated, and me yelling that if they didn't give me an epidural NOW I wouldn't be having any more children. "And I'm planning on having SIX MORE!!!" The nurses looked past the possessed woman in the wheelchair to the all-knowing fourth-year medical student for further instruction. Kevin said, "You'd better listen to her." I've never loved him more.

Joshua was not quite two years old, and Sophie only three weeks old, when "Kevin Gerard Hegewald" graduated from Eastern Virginia Medical School. Kevin's middle name is not Gerard. It's the letter G. Not the initial G because that would end with a period. Just the letter G. In an effort to look less German/more American, Kevin's mom gave him the middle name G in honor of her dad, Gerhardt. In an effort to look more German/less American, and to give a nod to his deceased Opa, Kevin had fabricated the scope of his middle name on the card he handed the announcer as he walked across the stage. It took our small cheering section a few seconds after hearing "Kevin *Gerard* Hegewald" to realize that we should be applauding.

Two days later, we packed up his medical diploma and our babies and moved across the country.

Orange Shag.

It looked perfectly planned on paper: two children born two years apart, four year gap, two more children born two years apart. But that four year gap was far from perfect. Sequestered between "starving medical student" and "finally a real physician" was the "survival mode emergency medicine resident."

Kevin and I were thrilled to move to the West Coast to have a California experience and be closer to our families in Utah. We quickly discovered that Loma Linda should not be considered a part of California. The delusional locals tried to convince us that the pea-soup in the morning air was a marine layer, but since we lived seventy miles from the beach, we were smart enough to know we were inhaling smog. The only advantage of the blanket of airborne pollution was that it made the scorched brown hillsides less visible.

We moved into a two-bedroom duplex and became the envy of all married students and residents because we owned a little piece of backyard. However, soon after we moved in, a flimsy wire fence was erected through the middle of the yard for two purposes: to keep a security dog in and Kevin out. We shared the duplex with a cranky eighty-year-old lady who had left her husband and was hiding from him. As if to prove all men are evil, on one of our first days after moving in, Kevin made the mistake of picking plums from a tree that was on "her side" of the property. Battle lines were drawn. She claimed the two-car garage for herself and left us to park in the driveway. That is, until she saw Joshua's brilliant sidewalk chalk masterpieces, which instigated her new habit of moving her car out of the garage into the center of the driveway each morning as soon as Kevin left for work. Apparently, living next door to a family with young children was not her idea of seclusion. Living next door to a cane-wielding wicked witch was scary enough; having to walk past her door to get to our own—terrifying. So I made getting safely inside our home a game.

Every time we pulled into our tiny remainder of the driveway, I would grab baby Sophie from her car seat and then time how fast Joshua and I could sprint inside. Unfortunately, having escaped one evil, I came face-to-face with another: orange shag carpet. The sight of it made me want to throw up. It looked like someone already had. No stylish furniture or chic decorating could distract anyone's attention enough to not be fixated on the hideous carpet. (As post-medical students we didn't have any stylish or chic furnishings. But the point is, even if we did, they still would have been an unsuccessful distraction.)

To top off our warm welcome to Loma Linda was hundred-degree heat, with no air conditioning. There were many times I believed I was going to die in this orange shagged hell. When our landlord came to visit, I had Joshua and Sophie lie placidly on the floor to look like victims of heat exhaustion. It wasn't too difficult to pretend; we all had sweat dripping down our faces constantly. Our landlord took pity on us, bought an air conditioning unit for the kids' bedroom window, and installed it by himself with an entire roll of duct tape. It was a brilliant strategic move on his part. From then on, I carefully considered before calling him if anything needed to be fixed. The term "doing a Zinsmeyer" became a powerful phrase in our marriage. Whenever Kevin attempted to take a short-cut in repairing something, I would only have to say the word "Zinsmeyer" and Kevin would put down the duct tape and reconsider his strategy.

Despite our surroundings, I was very happy in my mom role. I loved taking care of my babies—including all of the cleaning, feeding, bathing, reading, and diaper changing that went with it. These were the moments I had been waiting for my entire life. But I soon discovered that trying to be a super-mom could be a lot easier if I had a super-dad by my side.

I grew up in a home where my dad would kiss me goodbye every morning before he left for work. He would kiss me on top of my head and then with a loud "Hiya!" he would slap the same spot, to ensure that the kiss was pounded inside of me. Like clockwork, every night at 5:00 my dad would walk in the door and we would sit down together as a family for dinner. On Saturdays, he coached Little League football games, and on Sundays attended church meetings. He was a successful dad first and stockbroker second. My perception of the ideal family was built around having a dad who was present. Marrying someone with a physician's schedule wasn't the greatest idea to achieve that.

Emergency medicine was the perfect fit for Kevin. It offered him the excitement of not knowing what was coming through the door and the ability to leave the hospital at the end of a shift without wearing a pager. Kevin was excited to master the skills of quick decision making and knowing a little bit about everything. Unfortunately, it provided me with inconsistent night, weekend, and holiday schedules, and a husband with erratic sleeping and eating patterns. In short, his schedule didn't really complement my structured meal, play, study, and bed times. I struggled as much with trying to convince Kevin to carve out some family time as I did with potty training and binky-weaning my babies.

It wasn't his hospital schedule that frustrated me most; it was how he spent his time when he wasn't there. Kevin had this ability to pack in as much activity as possible in an unrealistic amount of available time. On his days off, he would wake up early and drive an hour away to Lake Arrowhead to spend the day bike riding around the lake and throwing in a fishing line at spots along the way. He enjoyed this so much that he applied for a night job at the tiny lakeside community hospital just so he could have the excuse to spend two full days playing, sandwiched around a sleepy night shift in between.

Close to the home front, Kevin signed up for any and all recreational teams—basketball, soccer, ping pong. (Those are listed in descending order of his natural talent.) He also divided his time between leadership positions in both work and church. But I definitely knew that family was not in the top priority spot when he volunteered to spend his nights in the hospital lab with pigs. Kevin jumped at the opportunity to participate in a research project that studied the effectiveness of a device that was created to help slow down rattlesnake venom from spreading through the victim. Kevin's job was to inject rattlesnake venom into live pigs, then try to save them, and document the results.

One night, Kevin promised me he would be home from the lab in time for me to leave the kids and be able to attend my monthly book club. When he finally snuck in at two o'clock in the morning, he was brilliant enough to have brought a fellow physician with him. Kevin claimed he didn't want his friend to drive home at that late hour. I knew better. With the friend spending the night, not only was Kevin rescued from me yelling at him, but also avoided having to sleep on the couch himself.

In case you're wondering, the results of the pig study were all negative. For four weeks, Kevin suffered pounding headaches from the loud squealing. Supposedly, his headaches continued when he came home to an irritated wife. (I might not have screamed as loudly as the pigs, but my words carried venom.) Ultimately the device that was the focus of the entire research project was proven completely ineffective.

We eventually visited a marriage therapist, once.

The conversation went something like this:

Abby: "Kevin is never home. Never. And when he is home, he's not really home. He fell asleep last week while eating his dinner. As I was talking to him! So I still had to put the kids to bed by myself."

Kevin: "I am physically and mentally exhausted after my day at the hospital. I need to be able to go for a bike ride or play basketball after work, but Abby refuses to let the kids stay up late so I can see them when I get home."

She called me controlling and Kevin selfish. We both walked out of there thinking, "We just paid her $200 to tell us something we already knew?!" We should have returned, but she was unable to meet during the hours Kevin was available—between 10 p.m. and 5 a.m. So I did the next best thing: I bought myself an expensive pair of running shoes. I took to pounding the pavement daily in the early mornings with a dedicated group of friends, and saved hundreds of dollars in therapy sessions. The five of us had a lot in common. Each of us were married to medical residents—two dentists, a podiatrist, a physical therapist, and a physician. Four of us had new babies at home. And all of us could run fast. Really fast. I'm realizing now the direct correlation between running fast and running from something. At the end of our six-mile runs, we would arrive home pumped full of endorphins, energy, and courage to face another day.

It was while running that I had an epiphany. A somewhat known fact in the medical world is that many physicians turn in their worn out wives for a younger model, and typically, the trade-in occurs right after residency—also described as the time when the rigors of medical school and slave labor of residency are behind, and paychecks are ahead. When I first heard of this trope, I felt sorry for the cast-aside wife. But increasingly, I came to view it much more as a win-win situation: the physician gets a new wife, and the old wife gets a new life with alimony.

Among my running friends, two marriages out of the five ended in divorce by the time their husbands' residencies were completed. Kevin and I almost tipped the scale. But I was still holding on to the hope that life after residency would get better. Without the added pressure of a chief physician always looking over his shoulder, and with a far less demanding schedule, I was convinced (well, not convinced but praying) that Kevin would choose to spend more of his free time at home. So in July of 2000, with our marriage hanging by a shoestring, we packed our lives, and my third pair of running shoes, and moved an hour west to San Clemente.

Looking back on the Loma Linda years, I have one major regret. For three years I was in a constant state of disappointment and anger at Kevin's inability and lack of desire to spend more time at home. I spent so much of my energy trying to change something I had no control over—Kevin. And I'm sorry that I didn't change the one thing I could have—that damn orange shag carpet.

Dress Rehearsal.

I am the recipient of two trophies. One was presented to me after running my first marathon. A survival tactic I created while running a marathon is targeting a runner up ahead. I steadily gain on them until I can eventually pass them before I lock sight on my next victim. Consistency is my strength. Uphill, downhill, it doesn't matter. My pace remains steady. Unfortunately, this includes the home stretch. In the final .2 miles of my first marathon, I locked onto a runner in front of me wearing a white tank top with the word *FLORIDA* in bright red letters printed on the back. I followed that tank top across the finish line. The next morning my dad picked up a newspaper with the printed results of the race. The first page included the top 100 female runners. I scanned for my time of 3:23:18 (Boston Marathon qualifier, baby!). There, at the very bottom of the page, in the 100th spot was … Miss so-and-so from FLORIDA. I had to turn the page to see my name printed at the very top of the list. #101. I hated Florida. My trophy-loving dad gave me a bronze trophy with a runner on top of it, but instead of saying #101, it simply said #1.

The other is a legitimate first place trophy for the seventh grade science fair. My friend Anne and I extorted all of the knowledge we could from my internist uncle and turned it into a blue-ribbon exhibit on diabetes. Our display became a popular attraction, not because of the gangrene photos of feet, but because we were doing hands-on testing. A short questionnaire screened students for predisposed signs of diabetes: "Are you always hungry?" "Are you always thirsty?" "Are you consistently wetting your bed?" Who answers "yes" to this type of stuff? I will tell you who: the prepubescent teenager who wants to have their finger poked by the cute girl holding a thumbtack so they can be given a bandaid to wear as a badge of courage. Obviously, some things have changed since my junior high school years. I am quite certain that randomly poking people with thumbtacks would now be considered hazardous. But one thing remains the same: junior high students have an ability to make dumb things look popular.

I could never have predicted that, as a young mom, I would be the one to recognize the symptoms and diagnose our five-year-old daughter with type 1 diabetes. Sure, Kevin was a physician. But it was me who handed a blood sugar tester to Kevin and told him to test Sophie. That one incident, and dozens since, have led me to adopt the belief that everything I have learned, I have learned for a reason. In my science fair research I had learned textbook information about diabetes—the symptoms, causes, and effects. What I was about to learn was the devastation of living with a disease that will never go away. My tenure as mother would now include administering multiple daily insulin shots, testing her blood sugar six to eight times a day, and forever being that mom who had to worry that a cupcake at a birthday party could send my daughter to the hospital. Some things I wish I didn't know anything about.

In May 2003, Kevin was diagnosed with cancer, just seven months after the discovery of Sophie's diabetes. But unlike the bucket of tears we cried with Sophie's situation, we were too shocked to even cry.

Cancer was not a foreign situation for our family. I have three younger brothers, and they are all champions in some way. Hyrum can put away thirteen hotdogs in one sitting. Matthew holds a record for career rushing yards on the football field. Quen is a champion at puking, having proven since his preschool years that anything from a winding car ride to having to touch the pooper scooper could eject the contents of his stomach. A few family vacations spotlighted Quen's talent—like the time he threw up on the Jungle Cruise at Disneyland, then spent the rest of the day with my dad in the air-conditioned "Tiki, Tiki, Tiki, Tiki, Tiki Room" lying on cots. My dad says it remains his best trip to Disneyland. A not-so-happy ending was Quen using my beloved Newport Beach canvas tote for a barf bag during a road trip to Seattle. I don't know which image was more traumatic: Quen trying to catch the vomit in his hands and it bouncing off and hitting the ceiling of our van, or my vomit-filled bag being disposed of in the nearest trash can. Needless to say, upon being diagnosed at age twenty-two, Quen puked his way through cancer treatments. It got to the point where the nurse only had to walk in the room holding the poison IV bags, and Quen would Pavlovianly puke in a strategically placed garbage can.

I learned a lot about dealing with cancer through Quen's experience. I observed how my mom decorated his hospital room with cards and photos of the family. And sent out positive newsletter updates to extended family, with pictures of Quen smiling in them. And how she always had two different meals prepared on treatment days so Quen could decide which one would taste just as good coming up as going down. Most importantly, I learned that life goes on. I watched in awe as Quen would endure chemotherapy treatments on Fridays, spend the weekends throwing up, and then get up and go to his university classes on Monday mornings. His professors never even knew what he was dealing with. Although I suppose they might have pitied his early onset balding. Unfortunately, Quen also demonstrated that cancer can return. Two years after completing all of his treatments, the cancer came back, forcing Quen to be hospitalized for a stem-cell transplant. But triumphantly he proved that if you beat it once, you can beat it twice.

When cancer swooped in to try to kill my husband, I couldn't believe that I was finally in a stage of my marriage that I no longer wanted to kill him myself. We were living in San Clemente. We had purchased our first home near the coast, and on a clear day we could catch a glimpse of the ocean if we stood on our tippy-toes in the corner of our backyard. Kevin was completely engrossed in saving lives in the emergency room at Saddleback Memorial Hospital. He worked eighteen shifts a month, which was six more than the average ER doctor, but that meant twelve days off a month to play outside—gardening, taking a long bike ride, or learning how to surf (his new obsession). He was still as active and over-scheduled as ever, but I didn't seem to mind as much because coaching the kids' soccer and basketball teams, as well as driving an occasional carpool, also made his agenda.

I was happily engaged at home with three young children—Joshua (8), Sophie (6), and Benjamin (18 months), with another boy (Sam) on the way. I spent time volunteering in my older children's school classrooms and organizing team snacks or making matching hair bows as soccer team mom. I had three marathons under my belt, but running now happened more for pleasure than escape. Most importantly, Kevin and I had learned the beautiful concept of compromise. He had enjoyed two trips to Alaska (without me), and I got two more babies. Win-win. Life was not without challenges, but life was good. Amazing how quickly that can change.

The large mass on Kevin's leg was identified as a malignant peripheral nerve sheath tumor. It took three weeks to get the official cancer diagnosis, and it took me three months to be able to say it correctly. Dr. Jeffrey Eckardt, an orthopedic oncology surgeon at UCLA, was our third consultation to discuss Kevin's options. We both felt confident that we had found the right man for the job to remove the tumor. Of course, this was because Dr. Eckardt was more focused on cutting out the tumor, rather than cutting off Kevin's leg, à la doctors one and two. After four months of a brutal chemotherapy schedule, and three weeks of daily radiation, all in an effort to reduce the size of the mass, the surgery was scheduled.

"Here we go Doc," Kevin said in his gregarious voice to Dr. Eckardt, the big man of the hour. Then in a more somber voice, "Jeffrey, I don't want to wake up without a leg. So if it needs to be amputated, I want you to wake me up and tell me first."

Dr. Eckardt shook his head in agreement. (He could also have been shaking his head at Kevin for calling him Jeffrey.)

Kevin continued, "And when you're in there, will you take a few photos on my phone?"

Because of that request I have pictures of Kevin's fileted open leg in my iPhoto library, and yes, they are disgusting.

"Here we go Doc." Now it was Dr. Eckardt's turn to speak. "Any music requests?"

Kevin replied, "It's got to be U2."

I'm not sure which U2 song lured Kevin into his anesthetized world. I hope it wasn't "Vertigo."

The surgery was a complete success. Kevin emerged minus one large mass and still the proud owner of ten toes. But despite the clean, cancer-free margins around the tumor, the UCLA tumor board recommended four more months of aggressive chemotherapy. Reluctantly, Kevin agreed. His life had been spared, his leg had been saved, and we were willing to do whatever it took to keep us from ever having to step foot in Dr. Eckardt's office again. And both of us truly believed that we would never need to. I suppose that is because I was naive, and Kevin was an eternal optimist.

Eternal Optimist.

At 4 a.m. on Martin Luther King Day 2010, our family of six stumbled into the car, eyes barely open, for an adventure. Kevin wanted to get an early start so we wouldn't be caught hiking in the heat. We made the two-hour drive to our destination and hit the dusty trail, with me wondering each step of the way how I had been persuaded to join in this outdoor experience. According to Kevin, this hike concluded with some amazing natural hot springs. We marched along the narrow trail, Kevin leading the way, assuring us one switchback after another that paradise was just around the next bend. In our final descent to the much-anticipated hot springs, I caught a glimpse of something that I couldn't believe I was actually seeing. It was like I was sixteen, watching *Thorn Birds* in my friend's basement, except in this situation, I had no desire to keep watching.

I quietly pushed my way alongside Kevin and whispered, "LOOK!"

His response, "Shoot. I didn't think they'd be here so early."

An explosion went off in my brain! Kevin KNEW that he was walking us right towards a nudist camp?! When the kids' pace dropped off dramatically, I could only assume they had also caught a peek of what I was seeing, and it wasn't pretty. Furiously I told Kevin we were turning around. But Kevin would not be deterred.

"Oh, it will be okay. We'll just go to that spring over there that's a little secluded."

Kevin never surrendered. He would rather go down sinking than admit a mistake, and he was not going to have his adventure ruined just because of a couple (or seven or eight) naked people.

As I sat fuming on the edge of the hot spring, Kevin and my properly swimsuited kids slid themselves into the steamy hot water. Our second of solitude ended as we watched with horror as a naked man came meandering towards us. Kevin bolted out of the hot spring.

"Don't come any closer!! We have kids over here!!!"

Undeterred, the man continued his approach and stood unabashed on the edge of the hot spring. I was horrified as I watched the faces of our four innocent children; their eyes were either glued on their dad or cast down, suddenly preoccupied with the water. The only image that could have been more mortifying at that moment would have been watching my husband fight a naked man. Gratefully, only verbal insults were thrown before the nude dude wandered back into the trees to find a different spring in which to soak.

This incident is classified in the Hegewald archives under the code word "nudies." Say the word and you will see my children squeeze their eyes closed, scrunch up their faces, and willfully try to dispel the disturbing images.

I had a hard time forgiving Kevin for this little escapade. I will be the first to admit that I am extremely protective of my children. Oh, who am I kidding? I suffocate them. But it was a challenging role being the only adult in our household who enforced wearing seat belts, helmets, and jockstraps. And if I was solely in charge, they would never ride in the back of trucks or jump on trampolines or dive off cliffs or ever leave the house. Which is why I hate to admit that life with Kevin was always more exciting. Did my kids feel safe and secure with their dad all of the time? Heck no! But did they have fun? Oh yeah. Everything became an adventure with Kevin. And my idea of adventure has never included hiking, dust, bacteria-growing hot springs, or nude people.

On our very silent hike out of the canyon, Kevin cheerfully said, "Well, hopefully our kids will claim the only time they saw porn, they were with their parents!" So as frustrating as it was living with someone who was stubbornly unpredictable, I had to admire Kevin's eternal optimism in any situation. He would need it.

The Day I Lost My Smile.

Once a year, I escape for a long weekend with five of my closest high school friends with the intent to laugh—a lot. In the early years of the girls' trip, we would leave typed agendas the length of novellas for our husbands to follow. A post-it note with an emergency number (that is not our own cell phone number) now suffices. With my husband, it didn't really matter how many instructions I left. Kevin did what all moms only fantasize doing by throwing out all scheduled activities, including school. He would load up the kids and a few sleeping bags, and the next phone call I received would be from the middle of a Joshua Tree campground.

But during girls' trip 2011, Kevin had different plans. With one foot out the door on my way to freedom, Kevin informed me that he was going in for a little procedure to investigate why his back hurt so badly. Kevin had been experiencing debilitating back pain ever since returning home from a family ski trip the month prior. He had investigated the possibilities of kidney stones or a slipped back disc but to no avail. Before I left, we played the twenty questions game concerning the procedure, with Kevin providing all of the right answers. Yes, he could drive himself. No, anesthesia was not involved. Yes, he would be home before the kids got home from school. And yes, I should walk out the door.

Although each girls' trip is in a different location, there are a few standard agenda items. We always visit the local grocery store and stock up on whole-grain bread, healthy cereal, and Greek yogurt, and then counter-balance our choices with fifteen bags of candy. Constant activity is the goal, whether hiking, playing tennis, biking, or walking, except when the sun is shining, which compels us to stop in our tracks and turn our faces towards the rays. (This sun-worshiping practice is ironically influenced not by those of us living in California, but by the friends living in Utah.) Five minutes of our trip are spent discussing our husbands, and the rest of the time devoted to talking about our kids. At night, we watch six hour BBC miniseries while devouring candy and admiring our fresh pedicures.

In 2011, my girls and I escaped to the ski slopes of Sundance, Utah. We gave reports on our kids while we rode up the ski lifts; systematically rotating friends to repeat the same stories that only best friends wouldn't object to hearing. It was during dinner that I used my allocated five minutes to discuss Kevin. I told them about his sore back and how I thought he was trying to pull a fast one on me by going in for back surgery while I was away. I imagined, in his mind, the timing was perfect—he already had three days off of work, and I wasn't around to bother him.

Three days later, when I returned home recharged, my life changed forever. Only Kevin met me at the door. I was expecting to be plowed over with the hugs and kisses and noise demonstrating sheer relief that Mom had returned home. Instead, silence.

Kevin pulled me into his study.

"The cancer is back."

"What?"

"The procedure I went in for was a biopsy, and it shows the same cancer cells as eight years ago."

"What?"

"I already told the kids. Just an hour ago at the dinner table. I probably should have told them after dinner because they all went to their rooms without eating."

"What?"

"I'm sorry."

I melted into a heap on the floor. I felt so upset and betrayed that he had withheld this information from me. But I knew that my anger was not only at the injustice of the world, but it also stemmed from my guilt of Kevin having to carry the news of this burden privately for three days.

My anger and guilt quickly melted into devastation. I allowed myself to sob uncontrollably that first night. I cried with the fear and frustration of having to deal with another year of a life completely absorbed by cancer treatments, and I cried with the thought of losing this man who loved me so much that he had allowed me—fully predicting his own situation—to go on my girls' retreat. It truly was perhaps the kindest and most unselfish thing Kevin ever did for me. That girls' trip might have been the last time I really laughed.

Sequel.

I don't mind repeating some experiences. Thanksgiving dinner, for one. Celebrating my birthday on the beach, singing Handel's *Messiah* with the church choir, and rereading *To Kill a Mockingbird* every few years, to name a few more. But driving back to Los Angeles to meet with Dr. Eckardt was more like watching *Miss Congeniality 2*—proving that there is no such thing as a good sequel, despite how well the first one may have turned out.

Here we were again, eight years later. I can't say that we didn't think cancer would never be in our future again. To be declared "cancer free" is misleading. Once you've been a cancer victim, you are never really free from it. Whether it's assuming every suspicious lump, bump, or itch must be cancer, or knowing that one day you will suffer the consequences of having had your body pumped full of toxic poison and radioactive materials. The fact that Kevin's hair never fully grew back from Cancer Round One proved that the effects were still lurking within. But we never could have imagined that we would be faced with the exact same cancer cells. Except this time, they were no longer neatly packaged in a tumorous mass. An MRI revealed that the cancer cells had metastasized, invading the nerves and bones throughout Kevin's back, shoulder, ribs, leg, pelvis, and skull. So the question we were asking was not, "Why?" but "How?" How did this widespread invasion happen as we were going about living our lives?

Still, the most shocking part of meeting with Dr. Eckardt again was the fact that he didn't remember us. For the past eight years, we had revered the name of Jeffrey Eckardt as the one who acted as God's hands, extending Kevin's life. We learned oncologists don't care as much about who or why or how. They accept their cases for what they are and focus their attention on what to do about them. And as an orthopedic oncology surgeon, Dr. Eckardt knew there was nothing he could do about this. After a five-minute office visit, he picked up the phone, called Dr. Sant Chawla, the oncologist who determined Kevin's chemotherapy protocol in 2003, and told him he was sending us over.

I will confess that Kevin, being a physician himself, got preferential treatment. I totally acknowledge that. I will also confess that I never felt guilty about it, although I sure feel sorry for the rest of the world. What might have been weeks waiting for appointments was for us typically just a matter of days, sometimes mere hours. But even with all of the special treatment, I came to the conclusion that it wasn't just because Kevin was a doctor—it was because he was a nice doctor. And more importantly, a nice person.

I can't imagine how difficult it would be to have a profession where you don't have much reason to smile. I remember looking at Dr. Chawla's kind yet expressionless face as Kevin and I sobbed from the other side of the big wooden desk separating us from him. I guess it would be grossly inappropriate if he were to say, "There's not much we can do," while sporting a huge grin. But I hope he has a very happy life outside of work. I hope he goes home and smiles and laughs all night long until it hurts, so when he reports back to work the next day he is relieved to have a break from smiling. Fact: smiling is not a prerequisite for an oncologist. Nor is liking your oncologist. But completely trusting them is. We were fortunate enough to not only trust Dr. Chawla, but like him as well.

On our first scheduled treatment day, Kevin walked in looking like the essence of good health, forcing all of those in the office to try to figure out which of us was the cancer patient. One of the Being a Physician Perks was being escorted to the private back room with the large, leather VIP chairs—one for Kevin and one for me. This also might have been to avoid some confusion from the other patients if they were to see Kevin inserting his own IV. (Which he never did, but he would have liked to.)

All you have to do is look around at a full office of chemo-sucking patients to be quite convinced that half of the world has cancer. It's a sobering yet inspiring sight to see a room full of people fighting for their lives. You see it all; cancer has no boundaries. But I will never forget one particular patient. He must have only been eighteen or nineteen years old and his body was covered with tattoos. It was hard to determine if he had had a hard life, or if the cancer had made his life hard. Maybe both. His body was emaciated. He was so thin that his jeans hung down below his boxers, which may have been the style, but regardless, he didn't have any meat on his bones to keep them up. He shuffled when he walked, with so little gusto I wondered if one day he'd decide that pushing through that door for one more treatment was just too much effort. He was always alone. Never a friend or a parent with him. Someone must have picked him up at the curb because there was no way he was capable of driving. Just looking at that young man and his valiant fight would cause Kevin and me to fall silent. I never imagined that only six months later, the image of this young man would flash in my mind as I stood looking at my own husband.

No Mountain Too High.

Kevin loved to give nicknames to everyone he met. He wasn't the greatest at remembering people's names, so he would just assign them a nickname, and in his brain, it stuck. But for most, giving them a nickname was a show of endearment. Josh became J-bird, Eric—Uncle Rico, Matthew—Mattius, Adam—A-burn, Tayler—Tay, Rachelle—Roach. The list goes on and on. I only heard one person decline his nickname, and it was a good call; no gentleman named "Jerry" should have to answer to "Geraldine."

Along with nicknames, Kevin loved creating mottos and battle cries. A bicycle race to raise money for Multiple Sclerosis research became "We Ride for Glory!" A fly fishing trip with his brothers earned the title, "Rod Benders." Much to my chagrin, a hunting group for rabid hogs became known as "The Hogslayers." Kevin affectionately called his group of high school best friends the "Awesome Sixsom," and his Sunday school class of seventeen and eighteen-year-old boys, "My Brothers in Arms." So it was totally appropriate, and expected, that Kevin would come up with a battle cry for this new challenge: Cancer Round Two. The decision was made: "No Mountain Too High."

If there was a motto Kevin lived by until that point, it was "Work hard, play harder." And there was no place he liked to play harder than in the mountains. In the winters of his youth, he skied them; in the summer he biked and climbed and scaled them. I don't know which he liked more—the going up or the coming down. I do know that he felt closer to God when he was in them.

His mountain adventures continued into his adulthood. His favorite involved hiking up several thousand feet in snow with a pair of skis strapped on his back and then precariously skiing down. In March 2010, Kevin successfully mounted the top of Mount Shasta in Northern California. I proudly included a photo of Kevin on top of the world on our family Christmas card. Kevin was horrified to overhear me tell an inquiring friend that it was a picture of Kevin on top of Mount Everest. He pulled me aside and explained that I would definitely have known if it was Mt. Everest … because he would have been gone for three months! Obviously, I am not a mountain girl. But I am so grateful that he chose "No Mountain Too High" for our cancer-fighting journey. Other options included "I'm Not Dead Yet" and "Cancer is the Craps." Leave it to our fourteen-year-old daughter to point out that as funny as the Monty Python skit "Bring out your dead!" might have been when he was diagnosed, it might not be so funny later.

The "No Mountain Too High" theme was completely embraced by our community of supporters. It appeared on a beautiful hand-stitched quilt and on elegantly printed notecards we were gifted. I can't imagine sleeping under a quilt with "I'm Not Dead Yet" embroidered on it, or sending thank you notes embossed with "Cancer is the Craps."

Although I can't distinguish between Mount Shasta and Mount Everest, "No Mountain Too High" became the title of a blog I started to report the details of Kevin's fight with cancer. I had never had the intention, or desire, to write a blog. I'd never even read one before. But just because I hadn't read one didn't mean that I couldn't guess that cancer was one of the worst subjects to blog about. But I like a good challenge. If Kevin was going to be fighting for his life, I could at least attempt to fight for the right words to document it. With the assistance and encouragement of a dear friend, I hesitantly entered the blog world.

My first post detailed the discovery of Kevin's cancer. I quickly realized the advantage of only having to divulge the painful details once. I could now ignore the phone calls of inquiring friends guilt-free. My blog was flooded with comments of concern and support, but one comment in particular jumped out: "Your blog had me crying and laughing at the same time." With those words, I found my inspiration. I became a woman driven by the desire to take a heart-wrenching situation and find the humor in it. If not for my own sanity, for my readers'.

For the first six weeks, I blogged the sorry details of our lives consumed by cancer. I described Kevin's attachment to a "man purse" filled with an experimental chemotherapy drug; enduring the Chinese water torture experience of CyberKnife radiation; of puking up Indian food while working in the ER. But then it happened. I had thrown it out for all of my readers to know that Kevin would be going in for a bone scan and MRI to determine the progress of the drug. BIG mistake. The test results were devastating. None of the tumors had shrunk; in fact, some had grown larger. The drug treatment was declared unsuccessful, yet the only plan was to continue on the same ineffective drug for six more weeks. I had been defeated; I couldn't even pull on my fake smile. There was no humor to be found in the situation. Nothing. Nada. None. Not only was I shattered by the disheartening news, but I was actually stressed out about how I was going to share it with Kevin's fan club.

Two days later, I channeled my inner Charles Dickens (who seems to write a lot about human suffering) and declared on my blog that our "great expectations" had not been met. I then took it a step too far (according to my mother-editor) and declared that my faithful blog followers should not expect any more posts from me. Later that same day, I retracted my resignation. I knew I couldn't give it up, no matter how difficult it was. Kevin wasn't throwing in the towel; how could I? And I had made an amazing discovery: the process of writing about the very thing that was breaking my heart was somehow helping to mend it.

Reality.

A few weeks before being diagnosed, Kevin walked into the kitchen and announced, "I just had the best dream!"

"Uh-huh," I responded.

Undeterred by my lack of enthusiasm he continued, "We were forced to spend every living minute with each other."

"That sounds more like a nightmare," I jokingly retorted.

I tried to dismiss the so-called best dream but something prompted me to ask,

"What color was my hair in your dream?"

"It was long and gray."

I was content, believing that Kevin's dream would play out sometime in the future.

Unfortunately, Kevin's dream came true all too soon. Spending every living minute together quickly became our reality. My days were now consumed with Kevin's situation. We had considered, for a brief, admittedly delusional moment, attempting to handle this challenge on our own. All too well did we remember Cancer Round One becoming a community service project. But we were advised by our local church leader that this experience was not meant to be ours alone. Little did we know at the time how very true this was. I have a strong belief in a God who is intimately interested in the details of our lives. He promises us that He will not leave us alone in times of need. He must have meant that quite literally because once the cancer news was out, we were never left alone. Our house was in a constant state of commotion with devastated well-wishers.

I have come to the conclusion that when friends don't know what to say or how to say it—they bake. Our family was inundated with homemade cookies, brownies, cupcakes, muffins, bread. Anything that could be wrapped, boxed, foiled, and left on a doorstep was. Most of the goodies delivered to our door couldn't be eaten by our gluten-free daughter, and shouldn't have been eaten by our cancer-fighting patient. And as much as I would have liked to enjoy them, my stomach was permanently lodged in my throat. But our spirits were fed. Well, and my three boys who gratefully devoured every one of those treats.

In general, all Californians anxiously await the next natural disaster to test their emergency preparedness skills. The church we belong to breeds a particular congregation of crisis squadrons. Just like the Red Cross, our church stormed in, prepared and willing to serve and lend aid in any way. The first rescue item on their agenda: providing meals for our family. With the special dietary needs of both Sophie and Kevin, I originally felt it best to keep this responsibility to myself. I lost that war. Meal dates were assigned to good-hearted neighbors and friends who accepted the challenge to deliver healthy, gluten-free dinners to our doorstep three times a week. It ended up being a win-win: I was able to spend more time with my family, and they developed an appreciation that they didn't have to cook gluten-free on a regular basis.

Time to come clean. Thanks to my sister, and my friend, Carri, I had premade thank you gifts wrapped and ready in a basket by my front door. As a result, I would proudly hand a lovely dish towel or large chocolate bar with a thank you tag attached each time a meal crossed our threshold. I got all the credit for looking like I was capable enough to pull that off. But really, who was I fooling? I'm sure the recipients realized that if I was capable enough to create a premade thank you, then I probably would have been capable enough to make our own meals.

One particular week I had to put out an SOS to Wendy, the women's group president in our church, to come rescue us from drowning in strawberries. There was an amazing strawberry sale somewhere, and we had been treated to strawberries and fresh cream, strawberries and homemade granola, strawberry shortcake, pints of strawberries for eating, pints of strawberries for dipping. Now an abundance of something would typically not be a crisis situation—I have no problem throwing any excess away. But, my mother-in-law was visiting. As in, my mother-in-law who grew up in East Germany where food was scarce and appreciated and definitely not disposed of. So I put Wendy to work—washing and slicing strawberries to freeze for smoothies, dipping strawberries in chocolate, organizing containers of strawberries to be delivered to others, and, most importantly, distracting my mother-in-law so she wouldn't see me jamming good strawberries down the disposal.

Our family fully felt the love and support of our community. All of those fighting with us even shared a distinguishing accessory: a blue and green band on their wrists inscribed with the words, "Hope for Hegewald."

The bands were inspired by our neighbor Kelly. Because Kelly is one of those people who always seems to know what to do, she ordered four hundred bracelets to be given to all of the youth and youth leaders in our church. They became bands for Kevin's "Band of Brothers." With friends and parents wanting their own bands, a second order for four hundred more was quickly placed and slowly received, literally on a slow boat from China. The spread of "Hope for Hegewald" bands was far-reaching. I would catch glimpses of blue and green on the wrists of church friends, neighbors, hospital coworkers, school class friends, elementary school staff members and teachers, soccer teammates, dear friends, and friends we didn't know were our friends. We sent bands across the country to our parents, siblings, cousins, nieces, nephews, and anyone else who claimed to be related to us so they could join in wearing this outward expression of support, unity, and faith in hope. Unexpectedly, the bands became an amazing conduit to opening up discussions for my children during those first awkward weeks after Kevin's diagnosis. When asked about the band, they were able to say, "It says 'Hope for Hegewald' because my dad has cancer." It's an awful thing to say, but it's a much more awful thing to keep inside and not say at all.

When Did We Get So Famous?

No Mountain Too High. Sunday, March 27, 2011.

Those were the words of my nine-year-old after the umpteenth goodie was dropped off at our door. The words "thank you" have never seemed so inadequate. I wish there were different forms of "thank you" in our language. One "thank you" could simply mean, "thank you for kindly passing the peas," and another one could mean, "thank you for noticing that I put on makeup today," and then there would be a "thank you" that is the ultimate thank you, which means, "thank you for sharing our burden and answering our prayers and being a disciple of Christ." That's the kind of thank you I wish to express.

Thank you for your heartfelt and uplifting letters, emails, and texts. Thank you for the homemade soups, chilis, salsas, breads, and baked goods. Thank you for decorating my home with hearts, and plants, and happy flowers like hydrangeas, lilies, daisies, and ranunculus. Thank you for your thoughtful gifts that bring Kevin comfort—music, movies, books, blankets, and prune juice. Thank you for your gifts that help ease my burden—gift cards, and note cards, and paper plates, offers to pick up groceries, watch my kids, drive my kids, adopt my kids. If I don't respond, please know that your offer was appreciated, and try again! I just didn't need anything at that time and I just wouldn't feel right about putting my kids up for adoption. A special thank you to my sister Kim, and her daughter Rachel, who flew in on Delta's wings to rescue me from drowning, when I thought it might be physically possible to drown in my own tears. Fortunately, those heart-wrenching, soul-sobbing, desperate tears have been replaced with "happy tears." When the little boys caught Kevin reading a letter with tears streaming down his face, he quickly explained that these were "happy tears"—tears that fall when touched by a spirit of love found in the kind words and acts of others. These are really the only tears now that fall freely in the Hegewald home.

Last week, happy tears really fell when Kevin opened a letter from our nine-year-old niece, Olivia. Kevin always tried to convince Olivia that he was her favorite uncle, but Olivia was quick to tell him that that title was held by two other uncles (who couldn't possibly have been more fun, but, living closer, were definitely seen more often). The note read:

"To my favorit uncle Kevin. Kevin, I hope you fight your canser and I was just kidding about Russ and Ryan. You know how teasing goes."

I've learned that sometimes, fame comes with a price.

Rule Book.

Unfortunately, there is no rule book detailing how to appropriately react or respond to someone dealing with cancer. I obviously had no idea what the correct protocol was on how I should behave, act, talk, or respond. I was never handed instructions to guide me. But now I've learned a few things. So here is my attempt at some of the "unwritten" rules of important dos and don'ts for those who come in contact with someone dealing with cancer.

When making a phone call DON'T say, "Call me back." Sure. I'll call you back as soon as I find a free moment during this emotional and physical crisis I am in. Simply say, "I'm thinking of you." Those words speak volumes. If you are desperately wanting a phone call back, try offering something in return. "Hey, we wanted to drop off dinner tonight from your favorite restaurant." Or, "Just wondering if we could kidnap your kids for a few hours." Both of those guarantee you a return phone call. Just don't offer to come inside and clean toilets. The last thing people would want is for you to see their neglected toilets.

DO say something. If you happen to run into the afflicted person, say something. Anything. There's no such thing as saying the wrong thing. Just kidding—there is. Like, "You should be celebrating! He's going to be so much happier!" But if both parties understand that there really is nothing that can be said, then you will be forgiving of one another. I remember seeing a friend in the grocery store and privately pleading, "Please don't say anything, please don't say anything." And then when the friend walked right by, I thought, "I can't believe she didn't say anything!" So basically, you're damned if you do and damned if you don't. But for me, I'd much rather be damned for doing something. I learned very early on not to pass any judgment for comments that seemed a little offensive given the time or situation. I understood that the perpetrator wasn't given a rule book either.

DON'T cry, unless you are invited to cry. It becomes a very difficult task to comfort someone else who is bawling for the situation you are in. However, if the person you are trying to comfort is already crying, feel free to join in. Just don't over do it. I'll admit, I've wondered if I was born dysfunctional. My tear ducts must have been put on backwards because when I see someone else start to cry, I literally feel my tears go back into my head. So remember, if you don't see any tears when comforting someone in trauma, know that they might be working very hard to be strong. That, or maybe their tear ducts have malfunctioned.

DO send a note. There is something so exhilarating, almost addicting, about getting the mail and opening a thoughtful note from a friend. The fabulous thing about receiving letters is that they represent tangible proof that we are not in this alone. Don't worry too much about the preprinted sentiments inside of the card. I've read quite a few hundred, so I know first-hand that professional card writers try to cover up their inadequacy at finding the right sympathetic words with a whole lot of other crap. Your signed name is all that really matters. But don't ever compare losing a spouse to losing a cat. Unless of course your spouse was holding the cat when they both departed the world. (That comment is totally unfair because I hate cats. I have no idea if losing a cat is the same as losing a spouse. For all you cat lovers, I sure hope not.)

Fan Mail.

Our family received a lot of fan mail. Our most avid fan bases seemed to be the state of North Carolina and Saddleback Memorial Medical Center. Yes, half of them were medical bills, but the other half were wonderful words of encouragement. Both made us cry but for very different reasons. I would gather Kevin's stack of letters and place them on the kitchen counter so he could see them. I found myself perplexed when the stack of letters remained there unopened. When I asked Kevin about it, he said he loved receiving letters; he just had to wait for the right moment to open them. Not me. I took claims on any letter addressed to "The Hegewalds." I tore into them and could hardly wait to feel the love that radiated out of the envelope. Imagine my joy one day when a letter came addressed simply to "Abby Hegewald." It had just MY name on it. It was just for ME. I tore it open and read the first few lines before I put it back in the envelope and tucked it in my pocket. I now understood Kevin. I needed to wait for the right moment to read this letter.

It was from Taylor Florence. I don't know Taylor very well, but we share a common bond. We both know what it feels like to live with someone who is fighting for their life. I didn't know his mom. I wish I had. I've heard so many amazing stories about Julie Florence, and quite honestly, they all sounded too good to be true. But after hearing the same types of stories and characteristics repeated by the next person, and the next person, and the next person, I pretty much accepted them as truth. I remember hearing how she invited young mothers with babies over so she could teach her girls how to feed and change a baby. I was touched by that. I have an odd connection to Julie, and I didn't remember it until Taylor's letter came. When we moved into our new house and neighborhood in San Clemente, I was asked to speak in church, and I was kind of excited because I thought this would be a great introduction to the church congregation. That

Sunday, the church benches were only half full. There was an exodus of church members who had traveled to Utah that weekend for Julie's funeral. It made me think how many of these same people who loved and cared for Julie were now loving and caring for me. I had wondered how they were so good at it. It's because they had done it before.

Perks.

Having cancer does have its perks. For starters, you are given a "cancer card" that trumps just about everything. You want take-out Thai food instead of a tuna-fish sandwich? Okay! You want to watch National Geographic instead of Disney channel? Okay! You want to host the end-of-the-season soccer party in our backyard? Okay! Kevin flashed his cancer card like he was auditioning for an American Express commercial. I don't remember the cancer card being nearly as powerful the first time he was awarded it. This was probably because I was pregnant, and anyone who's smart knows a pregnant woman is the only thing that trumps the cancer card.

Another perk is everyone's willingness to provide anything you need. One day while sitting in the oncologist's office, we received a text from a neighbor. "Can we get you anything?" I couldn't think of a single thing other than a new life, but Kevin was always a man with an answer. "Yea, I could use some Mountain Dew and prune juice." (By the way, a toxic combination.) We returned home to twelve 2-liter bottles of Mountain Dew and six bottles of prune juice. I made a mental note to respond "Breyers vanilla bean ice cream" were they to inquire again what we needed.

Cancer elevated Kevin to celebrity status: VIP and MVP became titles he could get used to. The first spoiled rotten night was spent with his indoor soccer teammates and competitors at an L.A. Galaxy game. Complete VIP treatment included passes onto the field for Kevin and my boys to watch the players warm up, box seats to enjoy the game, and goodie bags with every type of Galaxy paraphernalia imaginable. Kevin even got a new pair of jeans out of the night's events, though that gift was more spontaneous. When his buddies picked him up and found him still wearing his scrubs from his ER shift, a quick stop into Ross provided him with a $24 pair of Calvin Kleins. Needless to say, the incredible night left Kevin on a Galaxy high for weeks.

The second event was being honored as MVP in front of the crowd at an Angel's baseball game. We have a neighbor who is a writer and nominated Kevin as a "real hero disguised as a common person." No offense to Kevin, because he was deserving, but she could have nominated a tree and the tree would have won. Terrible traffic (I know, shocking in Southern California) caused us to arrive late to the stadium for the pre-game stadium tour. However, the director didn't skip a beat and led the five winners away in doubletime speed around the entire perimeter of the stadium. By the time we saw Kevin walking onto the field, he was a panting, dripping mess of sweat. He wasn't walking too well those days at a normal pace; the top speed tour had done him in. But oh, how that sweat made him glow. As the announcer presented each of the winners, their beaming faces were flashed on the scoreboard. Fortunately, it was a screen big enough to contain Kevin's jumbo-sized smile. My children and I sat in the stands, surrounded by friends and neighbors, and screamed and cheered as if he had just hit a grand-slam and the fireworks were about to explode. Kevin later confided in me how he felt his "MVP criteria" paled in comparison to a US Navy Seal Cadet or a special education teacher. "And here's Kevin Hegewald … MVP because he has cancer!!!" What Kevin failed to recognize was that he wasn't MVP because he had cancer; he was MVP because he had cancer and still kept smiling.

Spot Welding.
No Mountain Too High. Monday, June 6, 2011.

Last week I attended an eighth grade awards ceremony for Sophie. I watched as fourteen-year-old boys and girls, when hearing their names announced, walked up to the stage, were presented a piece of paper, and then stood awkwardly smiling as all of their peers and parents stared at them. I realized a little sadly that this would be the last time I would see Sophie take the stage in middle school ... off she goes to high school next year, where the opportunities to take the stage to hold a piece of paper are almost nonexistent. I came home and told Kevin that our society has done an amazing job inspiring teenagers to achieve great things just for a six-cent certificate.

Now imagine my surprise with the following incident. Last Friday, Kevin completed his fifth and final round of CyberKnife to the skull. As we were leaving the office and saying our heartfelt goodbyes with no "see you tomorrow" attached, Kevin was presented a certificate. It congratulated him for having "completed the prescribed course of Radiation Therapy with outstanding courage and determination. It is recognized by our staff as an Honorable Achievement, and we would like to congratulate you on a job well done." This six-cent piece of paper with photocopied signatures and his name written as "Hegewald, Kevin" actually choked him up. It made me realize, it's not the paper. It's that someone has acknowledged that you've accomplished something great. Isn't that one of the nicest things in the world—being recognized. When I asked Kevin why he didn't get a certificate the last time he completed CyberKnife, he responded, "I don't know ... maybe you have to do it more than once." I think that's it. Anyone can get perfect grades or survive cancer or endure CyberKnife once ... but to do it twice, now that deserves a certificate.

Reunion.

Everyone needs a reason to keep living. For Kevin, it was a family vacation to the Outer Banks. A Cannon family reunion for the first week of August had been planned a year before Kevin's diagnosis. Once our lives changed with the Cancer Round Two announcement, every treatment presented and scheduled involved us counting out the weeks to see how it would affect our family travel plan.

My mom had secured the ideal beach cottage next door to her older brother's house. A local, he would supply our party of thirty-three with all beach chairs, surf boards, boogie boards, umbrellas, kayaks, beach toys, and cans of soda. This would be our first visit not staying in the McPherson family beach cottage. After surviving yet another hurricane, my mom's brothers and sisters decided to quit tempting fate and sell the fifty-seven-year-old beachfront cottage before it became just beach. Staying in a three-story beachfront house with air conditioning, an elevator, and a swimming pool helped ease our sentimental pain.

The time had finally arrived. We had all been dreaming of this week spent in paradise. As much as I love California beaches, my heart fully belongs to the white sand, warm waters, and beach grass of North Carolina. And the hopes of finding sea glass. I am a sea glass junkie. I had filled Sam's head with stories of finding all colors of sea glass—not just the typical green, brown, and blue pieces that wash up on the California shores, but the rare shades of orange, yellow, and red. And not the size of my pinkie fingernail like the hundreds of tiny pieces I had warlorded my children into handing over, but pieces as big as his fist. The "Atlantic graveyard" is a veritable sea glass goldmine from all of the sunken pirate ships and treasures, and Sam and I had all of the hope in the world that we were going to make out like pirates. So we packed our swimsuits, flip flops, sunscreen, prescription drugs, fentanyl patches, pillows, and high hopes, and traveled to Salt Lake City to visit Kevin's family before departing for our Outer Banks adventure.

The night before we were to leave for North Carolina, Kevin was in excruciating pain. He had rallied in order to extend himself at an all-afternoon Hegewald cousin reunion and by nightfall was definitely suffering the consequences. The pain was relentless, radiating up the nerves in his spine, and none of our typical troubleshooting treatments worked. We changed his fentanyl patches, administered pain medication, gave him a hot shower, and prayed and pleaded with God that his pain might subside. Yet the hours dragged on, each minute worse than the preceding. We both knew there was no way he could physically get on an airplane. I was faced with a difficult decision: whether to send the kids with my parents or to join them and leave Kevin behind. In desperation, I made a midnight phone call to my brother-in-law, an orthopedic surgeon by trade and a drug-dealer to the distressed relative by default. I read off the labels of the prescription bottles that I had packed and he determined an appropriate regiment of narcotics. Kevin finally found some relief and fell asleep, sitting upright in a large chair in his parents' living room. I positioned myself on the couch and was still looking at him several hours later when he opened his eyes and said, "What time do we need to leave for the airport?"

How Kevin survived a day of flying across the country is a mystery. Well, not really a mystery. He was so pumped with narcotics I was grateful the airport didn't have any drug-sniffing dogs. The kids all took turns pushing him through the airport in a wheelchair, and for the most part, he slept through the entire experience. In the few moments that he was not comatose, he entertained all of those within earshot with his far-from-lucid comments.

Scene: A traveling high school orchestra group primarily composed of Asians walks by in the airport.
Kevin (loudly): Do you know what Utah has a lot of? Asians!

Scene: While waiting on the airport curb, a lady takes time to put the final coat of nail polish on her toenails.
Kevin (loudly): I've seen a lot of things in my life, but THAT takes the cake!

Scene: A middle-aged woman in a rush steps in front of Kevin's wheelchair.
Kevin (loudly): After you, milady (while pretending to take a bow).

It was a miracle we arrived on the other side of the country. And with that came the fear: we're on the other side of the country!

Our first morning in North Carolina, Sam and I were up with the sun combing the beach for the handfuls of sea glass just waiting to be collected. We walked, and walked, and walked, and returned home without a single solitary piece of sea glass. Not even an ordinary green, size-of-a-pea token. Sam was devastated and burst into tears. "This is the worst beach ever!!! If there was a list of the worst beaches in the world, this beach would be the first!!" I wanted to cry with him. I wondered why God was already teaching us how to deal with disappointment. The only treasure I found that day was a box of 800 mg. fentanyl lollipops from the Walgreens pharmacy. I could at least make Kevin happy, unlike Sam. A few licks of this quick-acting narcotic would help take the edge off of Kevin's intense pain attacks. In fact, it was so fast, he would often be found sound asleep sitting up in a chair with his eyes still partially open.

If you were to ask my children what their favorite all-time vacation was, they would all respond with the summer of 2011 in the Outer Banks. And miraculously, they remember their dad being pain-free and happy—a big part of what made it wonderful. They recall spending time with their cousins, crab hunting at night with flashlights, building a crab habitat, racing down Jockey's Ridge sand dunes, shell shopping, and spending hours and hours playing in the ocean. Sam even came home with some sea glass, thanks to Uncle Weston, who allowed him to choose several very large and beautiful pieces from his own collection—the very collection that I had coveted as a child and blame for filling my mind with the East Coast sea glass possibilities.

But the highlight was our last night there when we had an extended family reunion with our East Coast relatives. The Easterners supplied the Southern spread and good manners; the Westerners supplied the noise and entertainment. Kevin came alive! He took the spotlight and spoke for ten minutes—teaching us all about climbing our individual mountains. He proved that being with family is really the best drug out there.

Searching for my own positive memories of this family week on the beach is much like hunting for sea glass. I was in my happy place, yet, it felt completely foreign to the relaxing, book-reading, basking in the sun experience to which I was accustomed. I spent my days focused on Kevin's comfort, nutrition, and pain control, and my nights fighting the demons of despair. I was not at peace—with my life or with God. The once lulling and soothing sound of the ocean waves breaking on the shore drove me mad—it now sounded violent, harsh, never-ending. I felt like I was drowning. Again.

I'm not sure I would have remembered drowning if my mom hadn't taken a picture of me right after it happened. I was eight years old and a huge wave crashed on top of me, which had happened a gazillion times before. But, unlike all of the other times where I popped right back up to the surface, the strong current pulled me down to the depths of the sea floor. It then proceeded to flip me over and over, repeatedly banging my head on the sandy bottom. As my lungs were about to explode, the ocean finally released me from my gymnastics routine to break free to the surface. I arose from the ocean hacking up sea water and looking like Medusa—my long hair sticking straight up, a tangle of sand, seaweed, and small living creatures. Thus, the photo opportunity.

The rapid decline of Kevin's situation felt much like this drowning experience. God was reminding me, just as the ocean had, that I was NOT the one in control.

One day as I sat on the beach, I watched Kevin enter a calm ocean, embraced by a brother on each side. I watched them hold him up as he staggered in to feel the rush of the salty surf on his feet. I made peace—just for a minute—with God. I admitted to him that He was in control. I guess accepting that knowledge was my rare piece of sea glass.

The Beginning of the End.

Several people have asked me, "When did you know that Kevin wasn't going to survive?" The way our family reunion began planted the seed; the way it ended sealed it.

When I think back on August 6th, both Kevin and I were spending the night not where we had expected. In our final days of vacation, the thought that loomed over our heads was "HOW are we going to get Kevin home?" At this point in time, Kevin had one functioning eye and two non-functioning legs. The simple acts of standing up and walking without assistance, let alone seeing where he was going, were difficult. And—let's be honest—he was totally drugged to relieve his pain. Recognizing the need to get Kevin home quickly to his team of doctors, my sister-in-law, Candice, spent hours on the internet researching flight schedules and making all of the necessary arrangements. It was decided that my dad would take a direct flight to California with Kevin and leave me with the children to use our round-trip tickets back to Salt Lake City, Utah. I handed my dad Kevin's bag of drugs and a schedule of when and what dose and sent them off with a lot of prayers and a huge "Good luck!"

Due to bad weather in our connecting city, the first leg of our flight home was canceled. ("Weather" now added to my growing list of things that I could not control.) I was stranded at the airport in Norfolk, Virginia, with my four children. The airline arranged a free shuttle to drop us off at a not-free hotel to sleep a few hours before waking up at 3:30 a.m. to return to the airport for an early morning flight. Not until we finally landed in Salt Lake City eight hours later did I discover where Kevin had spent the night—San Clemente Hospital. Miraculously, he made it across the country with my dad, but the day ended with a ride straight from the airport to our local hospital, where Kevin was admitted—not as an employee, but as a patient to get his pain under control.

When I heard the news, I spent an hour on my knees sobbing and trying to figure out the fastest way to get home to California. It was late. There were no flights until the following day, and as much as I wanted to jump in our van and start driving, I hadn't slept in a week and was emotionally incapable of making the eleven-hour drive home. God solved that problem for me via Darin Gilson. I had felt prompted to call Darin, who still lived in Salt Lake City. I had no idea how I thought Darin would be able to help me, but I will never forget his immediate response: "Let's get you home." Within the hour, I had my car packed up with kids and bags, and Darin and Susie were driving us through the night to San Clemente. A very different road trip than our adventure to Wendover so many years ago.

When we arrived home in the early morning hours, I couldn't work fast enough to get everyone under my roof situated so I could jump in the car and drive to the hospital. When I entered that room and saw Kevin all attached to tubes, lying in the hospital bed, I climbed up in it with him and bawled. This moment marked the beginning of the end for me. I knew that my life would never be the same again because I knew Kevin would never be the same. But even in the deepest and darkest part of my brain, I could never have imagined that just six weeks later, I would again be crawling up beside Kevin in a hospital bed to bawl. The difference would be, this time, he wouldn't be alive to cry with me.

Three important things became permanent fixtures in our home after Kevin was released from the hospital: a home-health nurse, a Dilaudid pump, and my mom. The best decision we made was turning in the fentanyl patches and lollipops to upgrade Kevin's pain management to a Dilaudid pump. Unlike the inconsistency of the fentanyl patches, the pump allowed Kevin to have a steady amount of narcotics around the clock. Of course, we were to take some of the blame for the patches being unsuccessful. Little did we know that each time Kevin stepped into a hot shower, he was rewarded with an extra rush of narcotic. Which would explain why after three to four hot showers in one day, his three-day fentanyl patch would seem ineffective. Oops.

However, the Dilaudid pump was not without its difficulties. One day Kevin was in excruciating pain and asked me to come see if his pump was working. When I looked at Kevin, his shirt was covered in blood. I silently freaked out, which means I said out loud, "Oh my goodness, oh my goodness, we need to get you to the hospital," and on the inside I was thinking ... well, I can't really write what I was thinking. With further investigation, we discovered that his pump had become unhooked, the tubing had filled up with blood and was leaking out. Kevin simply talked me through flushing the line with saline, sterilizing the attachments, and hooking the pump back up to the tubing. Just so you know, those are not tasks I have ever had to perform before. He said that the Dilaudid withdrawal he had been experiencing was one of the most painful things yet. Usually I can't relate. But the day my mom left after living with us for four weeks? I know all about withdrawal.

Having my mom live with us was like having a personal genie. The great thing about GG (my mom, or Grandma Gayle) was she knew all of the correct appear and disappear acts. She made all dirty dishes, laundry piles, unwanted Tupperware, squeaking dishwashers, cluttered cupboards, and obnoxious weeds disappear. At the same time she made delicious meals, necessary grocery items, school supplies, and happy children appear.

Josh and Sophie were grateful for GG's unfeigned enthusiasm for mythology, *The Great Gatsby*, and United States history (read: summer homework). Sam loved her willingness to work on puzzle after puzzle, and Ben appreciated her persuasive tactics to allow him to watch a PG-13 Harry Potter movie (only because she said she would watch it with him).

Of course, Kevin had his own genie, too. Suzanne was Kevin's home-health nurse and anything that he needed—Poof!—Suzanne made it happen.

"Are you comfortable?" (Read Suzanne's quotations with a charming English accent.) Poof! A hospital bed, commode, and shower chair instantly appeared in our master bedroom and bath.

"How is your pain?" Poof! Suzanne made phone calls to the oncologist, the pain specialist, the pharmacy, but only after plumping Kevin's pillow, covering him with a blanket, and placing a cool washcloth on his forehead. I think I was supposed to model her appropriate behavior; she was like my *Supernanny*.

Suzanne brought with her an amazing arsenal of resources. Every day there was a different visitor—a physical therapist to teach Kevin how to flap his arms and march his legs, an IV nurse to draw blood for labs from the comfort of his own bed, and a social worker, who I think was pretty much there to make sure I hadn't completely lost it. (Fooled her.) Watching the magic of Kevin's needs being met, I decided to throw something at her. Thanks to HIPAA laws, I was in a constant battle with our insurance company's unwillingness to talk to me instead of directly with Kevin. Within 24 hours of notifying Suzanne of my frustration, I had an actual hard copy of a form that allowed me to engage in exhilarating discussions with our health insurance on behalf of Kevin. That was real magic.

Beautiful.

There are so many thoughtful ways to express sympathy. When Kevin was sick, a friend of mine from high school sent me a stunning, handcrafted piece of pottery. With it, she included a description of the process for wood-firing a piece of clay. Each piece is placed in a kiln and the fire is stoked from one to ten days, 24 hours a day. No two pieces end up identical because of how the heat, flame, and ash that adheres to the clay affect the piece. She disclosed that her husband, the talented potter, had witnessed more than once a piece explode during the firing process. I don't profess to know anything from experience about crafting a piece of pottery, but I know all about the capability of a refiner's fire.

The refiner's fire is a powerful thing. I believe that the Master Potter—He who created us—understands perfectly the nature and capacity of our clay. And because of that, He knows which firing process will help us become the beautiful vessel we are capable of becoming. He also knows how much heat we can handle. Well, I assumed He knew this. As Kevin's disease rapidly progressed, the vivid image of me exploding into a thousand pieces permeated my mind. I questioned whether God had me confused with someone else—some other lump of clay—who could withstand the flames that seemed to be consuming me. Yet from this near-exploding state, Kevin and I recognized the changes that were taking place within; we were finally becoming the people we hoped the other person to be.

Kevin's dependence on me grew more and more as his physical capabilities were stripped away. A tumor in his skull destroyed his normal eyesight. A growing tumor on his shoulder cut off a nerve running down his arm, robbing him of his ability to type, text, and eventually feed himself. Tumors in his back confined him to a wheelchair. And developing nodules in his lungs strapped him to an oxygen tank. His body was ravaged by the disease; he was so thin that not only did his ribs and bones protrude out, but so did the tumors on his chest and shoulder. One couldn't help but notice the eerie physical similarities between a Holocaust victim and a cancer victim. But even though disease stripped away everything from him, Kevin never allowed it to take away his smile. It's an extraordinary experience to be able to see past someone's outward appearance to the spirit housed within. Looking at Kevin, I had never seen anyone as beautiful. Which makes it a horrible conflict to be grateful for the refiner's fire that seems to be killing you yet is molding you into something beautiful at the same time.

I got to where I could see the change in Kevin, but I was also starting to see the change in myself. Spending every minute with Kevin was no longer something I needed to do; it was something I wanted to do. Of course I still had my human moments. Keeping Kevin comfortable was a full time job. I would ask if he wanted his socks on, he would reply yes, and then the moment I finally had wrestled them onto his feet, he would ask me to take them off.

His quickly changing needs really tested my patience a couple of nights before he passed away. He was trying to communicate something to me with his limited ability. I interpreted that he wanted me to place a fan to blow on him. I turned the fan on. He told me he couldn't feel it. So I turned it up higher. He then told me to turn it off. This continued for several back and forths until I finally blurted out, "Which way do you want it?! On or off?" Kevin responded: "Yes." Finally, I realized that he wanted the fan to rotate so he could feel it on, and then off, on, and off. I did tell him I was sorry I got so frustrated about the fan. I don't think he even remembered anything about it.

Another night I had a major breakdown. I was beyond exhausted when a dear friend dropped by and asked if I would be available to escape to go see a movie with her. Ironically, the movie was *The Help*, which is exactly what I needed, on so many levels. Tears welled up in my eyes as I broke down and told her, "I don't think I will EVER be able to leave my house again." She kindly offered for her husband to come and sit with Kevin, but I explained that he only wanted me by his side. At this moment in time, I was still envisioning years of Kevin being alive—suffering, but still alive—with me by his side. When I closed the door, I remember these words entering my mind: "This will be but for a short moment." At first, I thought the Lord was talking about my suffering. I discovered He was referring to Kevin's.

My advice to my children before each piano recital is this: "Start strong, and end on the right note." I truly believe that if you do these two things, no one will remember all of the mistakes in between. I have thought a lot about this, and I have spent a lot of time wondering if Kevin and I will be held accountable for ALL of the mistakes (and there were lots) we made in our nineteen years of marriage. I've come to my own conclusion that I think not. As many mistakes as we made, we ended on the right note.

We'd finally gotten there. We both finally loved each other the way both of us had deserved to be loved all of those years. I couldn't help wanting to say, "See, I told you if you would just slow down." Just as I know he was probably holding back the words, "See, I told you I wasn't such a bad guy."

Having arrived at the anticipated climax of that fiery furnace, I somewhat expected the heat to back off a little. I was wrong. My in-laws moved in.

Kevin made the phone call. He told his parents he would like them to come visit. They said they would come soon. Kevin said they should come now. They had been involved each step of the way, but we knew that they needed to physically see Kevin to understand the severity of the situation.

Quickly I realized that my mom had made it so easy for me to serve Kevin. She kept my house functioning and my children happy. But with my mom leaving and my in-laws entering the picture, I was forced to share Kevin. They took their rightful place beside him, and I was relegated back to the kitchen and my kids.

Sharing Kevin those last few weeks was probably one of the most difficult things I had to do. I was so grateful when night would come and I would be able to have him all to myself. We'd talk a little while I positioned all of his pillows and then I'd lie on the couch next to his on-loan hospital bed and listen to his oxygen tank and the never-ending grinding of his Dilaudid pump. Every ten minutes my phone alarm would go off, alerting me to reach over and give Kevin an extra bolus of pain medication. The sleep deprivation was definitely reminiscent of the years I spent caring for newborn babies. But the lack of a good night's sleep was a price I willingly paid to have a few hours of Kevin all to myself.

Hair.

When I was newly married, I remember watching the movie *Ordinary People* on television one late night by myself. I can't recall any details of the movie, except one. A husband, distraught over the tragic death of his son, chastises his wife for caring what shoes he wears to the funeral. As the camera revealed the stony, unaffected face of the wife, I felt like I wasn't supposed to be sympathizing with this supposedly cold-hearted person; yet I did. Somehow I innately knew that people show their grief in different ways, and I was certain a mother wouldn't feel any less sorrow for the loss of her son than her husband did. So if I knew this, then why didn't he?! I thought I had uncovered a tragic flaw in the characterization of the story. More importantly, why couldn't he understand her issue with the shoes? She's a woman! We are created to care if our shoes match our outfit. It is this inherent genetic makeup that prompted me one night to call my hairdresser friend. If there was going to be a funeral in my near future, I needed to get my hair done. Just because Kevin wasn't looking his best didn't mean I shouldn't try to do a little something with myself.

If you happen to pay attention to the flight attendants as they deadpan their way through the emergency information before the airplane takes off, you are familiar with the advice that in the event of an emergency situation, when the oxygen masks drop from overhead, you are first to secure your own mask before assisting your children with theirs. This is a perfect example of what I did not do. In my own emergency situation, I forgot to fasten my own oxygen mask. I worried about Kevin first and my children second, which explains why I was left gasping for air and barely able to breathe for six months. Running, reading, eating, sleeping were all doings of my past. Oh, how I used to love those things! But Cancer Round Two was a situation I couldn't outrun, escape from, or pacify with food.

One of the reasons I love Laura Bush is because she was often reported to be seen reading a book in the corner during family gatherings. Whether she was trying to escape George or her in-laws is beside the point. I can totally relate. There is nothing I enjoy more than sitting in my house or on the beach immersed in a good book. Once Kevin was diagnosed, that desire and ability completely disappeared. I could no longer concentrate on anything besides my own miserable situation. Out of habit, I took a new book with me to Kevin's first chemotherapy appointment. While we were sitting in the waiting room, Kevin decided to forgo reading the pamphlets on the wall entitled "Nausea and Vomiting" or "Mouth Sores" and read my book with me. My speed reading skills were evident given how long I would have to wait for Kevin to finish before turning the page. In fact, I wondered if he was even going to live long enough to complete the 473 page book. Just a few pages in, I was convinced the title *Unbroken* was completely deceiving because this character was down-and-out-broken in my mind. I forfeited the book and Kevin adopted it as his own. A few weeks later I caught Kevin with tears streaming down his face, agonizing over the need to finish this book. I told him to quit reading it. But he cried out, "I can't! I have to finish because there has to be redemption!" I think Kevin found some in the end: the character survives.

Because my life was focused on helping my own main character survive, much like exercise, proper nutrition, and adequate sleep, hair appointments were not a priority. For six months, the only chemicals I left the house for were Kevin's chemotherapy. So after my pending-funeral plea for help, my dear friend Rebecca agreed to bring her salon to my kitchen for a late night rendezvous. Once all of my brown but soon-to-be-blonde-again hair was all wrapped up in pieces of tin foil, we visited Kevin, who was confined to his bed in the room next door. The three of us sat and talked in the still of the night, while Rebecca turned through the pages of Kevin's special "Dad Book."

The book was my sister's brilliant idea. While visiting us over Labor Day, she spent the morning printing out pictures and purchasing stickers so my children could spend the afternoon creating memory pages for their dad. Sam especially could hardly wait to give it to his dad. When they rushed home from school the next day, they were so disappointed to find Kevin in a drug-induced coma. He wasn't really in a coma, but no amount of deliberate noise or prodding could wake him up. When he eventually joined the land of the living, the kids climbed up on the bed beside him and listened to him read each page, ever so slowly and slurred. This was a surreal experience, as I witnessed it through the lens of the video camera I was holding. Before me I could see three children smiling. Josh chose to sit on the couch beside the bed, where he didn't smile but wept through the sound of his dad's voice reading. We sat and listened to Kevin respond to endearing captions such as "World's best dad" and "My hero" and "Someone I look up to." Kevin already knew he was those things, but it sure was therapeutic for my kids to say them to him one last time. As much as I'd like to boast of the strength it took for me to stand there and record this, Kevin once again proved that he was made of supernatural powers: he's the one who had to smile for the camera. I've never watched it again. I don't know if I ever will.

As Rebecca thumbed through the book, I remember a discussion that late night. Kevin kept giving my hair curious looks and I think the drugs and the foil in my hair were giving him a psychedelic experience. But Kevin agreed with Rebecca that I should write a book. Mind you, he was totally drugged out (which is a detail I tend to forget when I write this), but on I tread, grasping on to the thought that I am accomplishing something Kevin had faith I could do.

When my hair was done processing, Rebecca and I excused ourselves to finish up the hair project. With all of the foils out of my hair and my head bent over the kitchen sink, I could faintly hear the dragging of feet coming into the kitchen. Not imagining who else it could possibly be at midnight, I said, "Kevin?" I was answered with "Oh shucks. I missed it." And then the footsteps slowly dragged back out of the room. Rebecca and I were dumbfounded as to what Kevin was hoping to see. Maybe he was hoping to witness how in a world that seemed so upside-down, my hair could be transformed into something that looked right.

Journal.
Tuesday, September 13, 2011.

I had a dream last night. Kevin was in his hospital scrubs leaving for work. He took me in his arms and kissed me goodbye and told me over and over again how sorry he was to have to leave me. I woke up a little sad thinking, That wasn't a dream, that used to be my reality. *I then realized it's still pretty close to my reality.*

Make Today Count.

The President of our church (The Church of Jesus Christ of Latter-Day Saints) Thomas Monson said, "People facing death don't think about what degrees they have earned, what positions they have held, or how much wealth they have accumulated. In the end, what really matters is who you loved and who loved you. That circle of love is everything, and is a great measure of a past life. It is the gift of the greatest worth." He continues, "Time is a gift, a treasure not to be put aside for the future but to be used wisely in the present."

We read this quote on a Monday night during one of our weekly family discussions. Kevin and I knew his end was near, and we wanted to let our children know that, too. Not that they couldn't physically see it in their dad's appearance, but somehow the brain still refuses to accept that death will come. So we made a commitment to each other that we would make every day count. That became our newest family motto. I definitely missed the old days when our motto was "Work before play" or "Be nice." But I guess "Make today count" is a motto we should all strive to live by. Some situations just really encourage us to do it. We asked our children, "If today was the last day our family might be together in this life, how would you spend your time? What would you do differently?" There were a lot more hugs. And a lot more kisses. We've always said "I love you" a lot, but we made sure it was the last thing we said at the end of the night. We decided that as long as you can go to bed knowing that your family knows you love them, and you feel loved by them, then you can go to sleep confidently and peacefully.

With our new motto, Kevin faced the decision of how he wanted to spend his time. The answer came more as to what he didn't want to do … and that was to endure a painful drive up to Los Angeles to participate in a CoQ10 study. After we returned home from our Outer Banks adventure, we had high hopes that a new cancer therapy using

CoQ10 would be able to extend Kevin's life by a few months. Kevin loved the concept that CoQ10 would not only attack the free radicals that damage cells, but increase cellular energy in the good cells. The few patients we had met who were involved in the CoQ10 study all had one thing in common: they felt better. Unfortunately, Kevin didn't feel well enough to even get in the car to drive to receive the treatments that were to help him feel better.

So we stayed home. And we were blessed with ways to make each day count. One afternoon, Kevin was determined to go watch Josh surf. Kevin missed surfing. He missed surfing with Josh even more. Josh got a head start to the beach, leaving Kevin to follow with his good friend, fellow physician, and hiking buddy—who was also named Kevin. By the time K-1 and K-2 (as they called each other) finally arrived at the beach, after making a quick pit stop for some take-out hot and sour soup, Josh had already finished his surf session for the day. The waves were cruddy and the weather cold. But when he saw his dad painstakingly making his way across the sand, Josh stood up and started putting his wetsuit back on. It didn't matter that Kevin only lasted ten minutes sitting in a beach chair before feeling the need to start the tedious trek back home. Josh witnessed the effort his dad had made to come watch him, and he was happy to put on a show.

On Labor Day weekend, we were surrounded by fun and activity that my sister Kim and my brother Quen and their families brought into our home. I tried not to believe that the reason they flew in and drove down was to have their children spend one last day with their Uncle Kevin. Kevin was always his best self when surrounded by people, and he even took a spin in his wheelchair so he wouldn't miss out on seeing the movie, *The Avengers,* with everyone. We might have been watching superheroes on the big screen, but we were all more impressed with the one we were sitting with. (On a side note, our superhero was miserable and couldn't wait to get home, but no one would have guessed that.)

With September also came the first day of the new school year for my children. Sam was entering second grade, Ben fourth, Sophie was a freshman, and Josh would be a junior. As per tradition, Kevin gave each of the children a father's priesthood blessing to provide them strength for the upcoming year. That was a humbling experience as we watched Kevin require help to raise his arms to place his hands on top of their heads. Yet as we closed our eyes and listened to the words of his prayers, his voice was as steady and strong as we once knew his body to be.

I felt like time slowed down. In fact, the first day of school was painstakingly slow for Josh and Sophie. They spent three hours sitting outside in the stadium in record-breaking heat after one disturbed teenager threatened to blow up the high school. I guess not everybody is excited for school to start.

The next day our power went out during a rolling blackout, as it did for much of Southern California. I'll count myself among the millions who had been running their air conditioners on high. But having no power was a gift. (Except for the non-working oxygen tank for a few hours.) No TV, no iPad, no computer. Just all of us sitting around our family room lit with candles, telling stories and eating Carl's Jr. burgers that a neighbor had driven thirty miles north to buy.

As we continued to cherish and stretch our time, the number of visitors escalated. We had an invasion of Cannon and Hegewald relatives arrive throughout September, and I was grateful for neighbors who offered their guest rooms as an extension of the overflowing bed-and-breakfast I was running. When school was canceled a second day due to the power outage, my kids were able to spend the afternoon at the beach enjoying the cold water and the warm weather with both sets of grandparents.

We spent the weekend watching Sophie successfully conquer her first high school tennis match, Benjamin play goalie for the first time on his club soccer team, and Samuel run like crazy on the soccer field. An entire entourage was there cheering them on, including Kevin with a front row seat in his wheelchair. That night my brother Matthew had arranged to take Josh and my brothers, Hyrum and Quen, along with my dad, to watch the USC vs. University of Utah football game.

Even though Josh cheered for USC in the U of U fan section, it was comforting to know that my brothers would do their best to help direct Josh, and all of my kids, in their lives.

After surviving a harrowing week, which included blood and platelet transfusions and a heart-wrenching moment of signing hospice papers (Kevin and nurse Suzanne had been begging me for two weeks and I'd refused), the following Saturday was a repeat with a new cheering section. Sophie had a tennis match, Ben and Sam soccer games, and all of Kevin's brothers came to visit—Mario, Gordon, Andrew, and Markus, who is technically a cousin but regarded as a brother. Kevin was in charge of the day, which meant he was right there on the sidelines. On our drive home from Ben's game, Kevin said, "I'd love to go home and sneak into bed, but why don't we have my family come meet us for smoothies." So that's what we did. For the record, I tried to talk him into going home to bed. That darn cancer card won again. He even extended his evening by sitting outside around the fire pit in our backyard visiting with his parents and brothers. Well, his family did the talking; Kevin did the listening. He had perfected that skill.

According to Kevin, it was a perfect day. He had made the most of every minute, and he was content—with his life and with the world.

Crap Room.

The night before Kevin passed away, he slept in a chair. Of course, not any old chair, but his favorite chair. Ironically, Kevin can be called a lot of things, but never a lazy boy. This well-loved leather recliner had graced our home for the past eight years after my parents gifted it to him during Cancer Round One. Drawing on their own experience of taking care of my brother Quen during his bouts with cancer, they somehow concluded that if you felt like puking your guts out, it's nice to be sitting in a big comfortable chair. In Kevin's final weeks, this chair had become his favorite spot. It almost became his final resting spot. The chair had been moved from the family room into our temporary bedroom, and Kevin preferred sleeping in it rather than the loaner hospital bed.

Ever since Kevin decided to not use his limited energy to walk up a flight of stairs to go to bed, we had moved into our main floor guest room. The words "guest room" imply that the room was accommodating to guests. In actuality, the only thing accommodating about it was its proximity to the beach. The room was minimally furnished with a pull-out sofa, a small desk table and chair, a night stand, an artificial plant, and a closet filled with crap. Which is why I called this room our craft room in front of the kids and the crap room when they weren't around. Not until Kevin and I took up our new bedroom residence did I wish it had been furnished with a nice bed. (To all of our past visitors—sorry.)

I might have failed on the bed, but I nailed it with the name. Well, I guess that depends on how I choose to look at it. Kevin passing away in this room—perfectly named. The room becoming hallowed ground—pretty much the opposite of a crap room.

On Kevin's final night, I sat on my not-pulled-out couch bed and felt the presence of angels. Not only was I aware that they were there, but I knew why they were there. They were gathering to escort Kevin home. Kevin, being true to his outgoing self, spent the night talking to them. He would suddenly sit upright and start stuttering and babbling, working so hard to form words and to be understood. I discovered that if I responded in a way that implied I understood him, he would relax, his face would break out in a huge grin, and his body would collapse back into the chair.

I have no idea who they were. I could barely keep track of all of Kevin's living visitors, let alone the dead ones. But I sensed a familiarity with some of them. Earlier, Kevin and I had strong impressions that both of our grandmothers—Grandma Lorna from North Carolina and Omi from Germany—would be coming to escort him to heaven, and my Uncle Roger would be waiting for him just beyond. But I have no idea which of our dead ancestors loved the Jazz as much as Kevin.

I know this is going down as Hegewald folklore, but I am only reporting what I heard. Kevin was a big Utah Jazz fan, much to the dismay of his Lakers-loving boys. (The feeling went both ways.) Even after Stockton and Malone left, Kevin's loyalty remained. So when Kevin shot up in his chair with an enthusiastic "The Jazz?? Four … four times … in a row?" in an effort to help out both Kevin and the deceased Jazz-lover, I responded with equal enthusiasm, "Yes! The Jazz finally won four games in a row!" I was rewarded with a huge smile.

It truly was a miracle we made it through that final night. Kevin struggled to breathe, and he never opened his eyes or really communicated, at least with me. We had an on-call hospice nurse with us in the other room, but the only time I really needed her was when she had left for another call. But I wasn't really alone; I had my angels. I knew they'd stick with me until the end. Well, Kevin's end.

September 20.

5:00 a.m. Blog

Started the day with a post on my blog. However, it wasn't my post—it was Kevin's. He had been wanting to hijack the blog and post his thoughts on adversity, but his inability to type had left him unable. So I fulfilled that desire for him. I had no idea that I would be making another post this same day, announcing that Kevin's fight was over.

6:30 a.m. Get ready

Something felt different. So after my three minute shower, I took the time to do my hair and put on my makeup and pull on my favorite pink sweater with a black ribbon sash. I wanted to look beautiful if Kevin happened to open his eyes. He never did.

7:40 a.m. Kids to school

Security in routine. Walked Ben and Sam up the street to school. I told them, as I had told Josh and Sophie earlier on their way to early morning seminary, that we would call them out of school if it was time to say goodbye to their dad. I walked back into a house that was still full—Kevin's parents, brothers, and best friend all taking up space and taking turns sitting next to Kevin.

10:00 a.m. Phone calls

I called my parents and asked them to get on a plane.

Suzanne called the EMTs and asked them to come lift Kevin from the chair to the bed.

11:00 a.m. Rescue

I heard the EMTs arrive and chat with Suzanne as they were directed to Kevin. Once they entered the crap room, they fell silent. I think they felt the angels. They eventually made some kind remarks about how Dr. Hegewald had helped them many, many times when they had dropped off patients to the emergency room door and what an honor it was to now be able to serve him. Kevin moaned loudly when they efficiently but gently moved him to his final resting spot. I didn't know those men. But I love them.

3:00 p.m. Release

When my boys returned home from school, they watched two things: their dad dying and *Soul Surfer*. Recognizing that the time was close at hand, I asked our local church leader to come over and join us as we gathered as family and dear friends around Kevin's bed. We listened to a very touching and emotional blessing given to Kevin from his father—telling Kevin that he had valiantly done all that had been required of him in this life, that he could now depart this world, and that all would be well with his family. There was a very important person missing from this family circle—Sophie. Sophie was with the high school tennis team competing in a match in Irvine, thirty minutes away. Arrangements were quickly made for a brother-in-law to go pick her up. I texted her tennis coach to please let Sophie know it was time to come home.

3:30 p.m. Slow motion

Josh, Ben, Sam, and I stayed by Kevin's bed—sobbing and touching and loving him. My own indescribable grief was intensified as I watched my three heart-broken boys being racked with the deepest sadness over losing their best friend. Sam crawled up on the bed right next to his dad and stroked his arms. Kevin would moan a little when Sam moved around on the bed, and I was concerned he was in pain. But the slight smile in the corner of his mouth showed me that he was perfectly happy with Sam on top of him, even if it was hurting him. Josh knelt at the side of the bed, put his head down, and sobbed. And Ben chose to sit with his back against the bed, unable and unwilling to watch his dad struggle.

Each breath of Kevin's was deliberate, difficult, as he determinedly held on, feeling those four pairs of hands and knowing there was a pair missing.

4:15 p.m. Sophie returns

When Sophie finally returned home, everyone cleared out of the room so she could have a private moment with her dad and me. Sophie and I exchanged details of the events of the day as Kevin struggled and gasped, patiently waiting for his two girls to stop talking. When Sophie expressed her fear of being in the room when her dad took his last breath, I was impressed to have her leave the room immediately. At that very moment, I alone witnessed Kevin's final breath.

4:45 p.m. Time stops

I notified my houseful of people that Kevin had passed. I watched Suzanne as she noted the time, then took a towel and wrapped it around Kevin's neck to hold up his drooping head. She then turned her attention to his hands. Hands I had held for 20 years. Hands that had changed diapers, thrown toddlers in the air, pushed bicycles and lawn mowers. Hands that had built and fixed and destroyed and created. Hands that had saved lives in the ER. Hands that had been raised but also humbly folded to God. Now hands that were white and cold and rigid. I observed as Suzanne gently took those hands and uncurled his fingers to rest flat by his sides. My brain tucked this away.

5:00 p.m. Lasagna left on the front porch

Sometime p.m. Stillness

The night was spent with everyone rotating through the room to be with Kevin. My parents arrived from Salt Lake City and were able to sit next to him for one last time. I waited patiently for my turn to be alone with him. Finally my moment. I climbed on the bed and curled up next to Kevin. I didn't cry. For some reason, I couldn't. I was just still, wondering how much of me had died that day with him.

11:00 p.m. Silence

My house was filled with heartbroken non-sleepers when the mortuary came to take Kevin away. I had said good-bye to Suzanne, good-night to my in-laws, who were sleeping in Sophie's room, and good-night to my parents, who were staying in a neighbor's guest room.

12:15 a.m. Blog

I walked upstairs and ended my day with where it had started: sitting at the computer posting on my blog. I then entered a bedroom I had not slept in for eight weeks. I crawled into bed next to Sophie, relieved that I didn't need to be alone and grateful that, for fear of waking her, I couldn't cry in my bed all night long.

I closed my eyes.

When I think about September 20th, I feel love. I heard an elderly father profess his love to his son. I witnessed a dying father's love for his daughter; he showed how much he loved her by waiting for her. And I felt the love of my Father in Heaven, who sent angels to our home that day. I came to recognize that angels were not just there for Kevin but for me and each of my children, too. It was in these moments that I grew a deeper understanding and a profound appreciation for the Savior's Atonement. I am forever grateful to Kevin for making this experience beautiful for me.

The Fight Is Over.
No Mountain Too High. Tuesday, September 20, 2011.

He fought the good fight, he finished the course, he kept the faith.

At 4:45 p.m. tonight our dear husband, dad, son, brother, and friend returned to his heavenly home.

How grateful we are for the knowledge we have that he still lives.

Thank you to all of you who have climbed this mountain with us. I love you.

Kevin, you will be missed.
Abby

Haunted.

I grew to hate nights. I would stay up as late as possible, with the hopes that when I crawled into bed I'd fall fast asleep. But no matter how late it was, my thoughts were haunted. The image of Kevin gasping for air in the final hours of his life would become vivid in my mind. Just as disturbing was my inability to think of the last conversation we'd had. The last *real* conversation. One that mattered. Not one about what he wanted to eat for lunch, or if his pillows needed adjusting, or anything to do with managing his pain. Of course we'd had many important conversations over the past months—my financial future, whether I should stay in California, funeral arrangements. But my mind was searching for a conversation that was proof that everything was alright in our relationship—that I hadn't imagined being crazy in love with this man who was crazy enough to love me back.

Our last argument certainly came to mind.

I was driving Kevin to a radiation treatment and recounting the conversation I had with Josh earlier that day concerning how he should handle a potential job and his new employer. I can't remember the details of the advice I gave to Josh, but apparently it wasn't the best.

"Josh really shouldn't be making demands before he's even gotten the job," Kevin kindly pointed out.

I lost it! The fear that I physically fought every day reared its ugly head—not just the fear of being left alone, but the fear of being terribly inadequate and incapable of handling life, and my children's lives, and all of the thousands of decisions that would demand to be made—I would have to make all on my own. Obviously the situation that day wasn't the first time I had messed up. There's a reason Kevin and I jokingly referred to our savings account as a "therapy fund" for our children to use in the future. But the reality was, without Kevin, I was going to mess up a whole lot more. I just longed for Kevin's vote of confidence; I needed to know that he thought I was going to do just fine … even if I wasn't. This was one of those times I wouldn't have been upset if he'd lied.

I do recall two conversations—ones that really mattered—in Kevin's final days. That is if you consider two lines a conversation. The first occurred when I looked at him resting on his bed. Not really resting, enduring. The realization flooded over me that Kevin was truly doing just that. He knew he'd been beaten. He looked like he'd been beat up. And yet the expression on his face was complete acceptance. No anger. No fear.

I remember asking him something, knowing full well that his answer would hurt me. I pushed the lump down in my throat. "You're excited to leave, aren't you?"

"I really am."

The sorrow and grief that had filled my entire soul allowed compassion in. That's a positive about cancer: when you see someone you love suffer as much as they do, you are willing to let them go. And I knew if Kevin was actually okay with leaving us behind, and looking forward to where he was going, then I needed to let him go.

The other conversation took place in a moment of despair, late in the night. I put my head down on his chest and whispered, "I am going to be so lonely." It wasn't said with self-pity. It was just stating the obvious.

Kevin's response was immediate, calm, and deliberate: "Abby, I promise you that you won't be."

This is the part in the conversation where I was supposed to respond with "How do you know that?" What was he referring to: my children, my friends, a new spouse? I don't know. I do know that he wasn't really in the position to make such a promise, but I didn't ask him because I didn't care. I just wanted desperately to believe him.

I might as well point out that he was wrong. I do feel lonely. A lot. I've learned that being "alone" and "lonely" are two different things. With four children and friends and family I am close to—I am never alone. But sometimes I have felt the loneliest when surrounded by people. Maybe that's what Kevin thought I said—"I'm going to be so alone." Or maybe this time, he'd learned from our last argument's response, and he lied. I suppose a good-intentioned lie is sometimes the kindest answer.

We never really said the word *goodbye*. But we did say "I love you." Lots. Those were the last words he heard me say. And I'm alright with that because I think that's *much* better than goodbye.

Deadlines.

The morning after Kevin died, I was faced with deadlines. I've never seen the humor in that word until I just wrote it. That's hilarious. It's like I'm describing myself looking in the mirror. Actually … I had a long list of decisions that needed to be made, but at the top of the stressful list was writing and submitting the obituary to the local newspaper by 2:00 p.m. Up to this point, I had never really read the obituaries. I am now a faithful obituary follower. In the hundreds of obituaries I have since read, I have come to the following two conclusions:

1. Most people are really old when they die.

2. No one dies and has a funeral only four days later.

Since Kevin passed away on a Tuesday, in order to be printed in the paper on Friday, announcing the funeral on Saturday, the article had to be submitted by Wednesday. I really do recommend having your obituary written in advance. In fact, start right now. I've already started writing mine. Most of it focuses on my role as a mother, with a list of positive, acceptable adjectives that my children can choose from to insert.

I also needed to meet with the mortuary to discuss the burial arrangements. I took both my parents and my in-laws, with the hope that between the five of us, one of us would have a clear head. Thankfully, because of some strange, yet good advice from my aunt, we had done our research for a casket on Costco.com and came prepared. The mortuary offered the exact, beautiful, dark wood casket we had already selected, slashed the price $3,000 to match Costco's, and saved me the fear of not having it arrive in time—or showing up at my front door—both equally frightening prospects.

An unfortunate thing happened at the mortuary. (Actually, I wonder if anything fortunate ever happens there?) When I asked for the shirt that Kevin was wearing when he passed away, they returned it to me in pieces. Kevin happened to be wearing a t-shirt from Doumar's in Norfolk, Virginia. Doumar's is famous for its drive-up dining, limeades, and "double dogs," which consists of a hot dog sliced in half lengthwise and served on a hamburger bun. Fine dining. Obviously, I didn't put a whole lot of thought into what Kevin was wearing the day he died; we were going for comfort, thus a pair of athletic shorts and an oversized t-shirt. Nonetheless, I was devastated to be handed a cut-up shirt. My mom later called back East and explained to the owner that her dear son-in-law had died wearing his beloved Doumar's t-shirt, which had been heartlessly destroyed by the mortician. The owner was of course very sympathetic. How couldn't he be? Can you imagine the compliment that someone died wearing one of your ten dollar t-shirts? If the timing hadn't been so inappropriate, I'm sure he would have asked for a photo of Kevin wearing the shirt so they could hang it on a plaque on the wall, right next to food critic Guy Fieri, with the inscription "Doumar's is to die for." But thankfully the tactful owner didn't ask. One week later, I received a package with a replacement t-shirt and enough Doumar's stickers to wallpaper a bedroom.

Next big item on the deadlines list was deciding the funeral details. Kevin actually helped plan his funeral … or should I say funerals. The idea was to have a formal funeral in San Clemente where we lived, and a less-formal gathering, or "celebration," in Salt Lake City where he grew up. Call it whatever you want—if you gather together in a church with a casket front and center and you start and end with a prayer—it's a funeral. A few weeks before Kevin passed away, I sat next to him to discuss the details. We created a list of family members and friends to give tributes and prayers. The music for the services was a little more difficult to finalize as Kevin's requests included the less-familiar hymns "Lead Kindly Light" and "If You Could Hie to Kolob" as well as songs by U2 and The Alarm. Kevin gave his suggestions, but I don't think he really cared. We both knew that the person left behind gets the final say. What Kevin really wanted was to be cremated and then to have a paddle out in the ocean to spread his ashes, as many surfers do.

So he was just humoring me, responding to this funeral stuff. I imagine if I had died first, I would be riding the waves to Asia right now.

I met with our church leader who would be conducting the service and turned over our proposed agenda, giving him the assignment to contact each participant with the "good news" that Kevin wanted them to speak at his funeral. I became an expert at turning things over. Never before had I been so grateful for my delegating skills, or my circle of talented friends that I could impose on. I sent out an email saying, "It's time to plan a party." Then one by one, I checked off the needed services by assigning the perfect person for the job.

Flowers for the casket, boutonnieres for the pallbearers—Dave.

Funeral program typed and printed—Stacey.

Guest book for the funeral—Carri.

DVD of Kevin's life—Michael and Ken.

Display of photos, Kevin paraphernalia in church foyer—Su.

Photographer—Elizabeth.

Video recorder—Wayne.

Makeup, hair, and wardrobe—Rebecca.

Open house & refreshments for 500 guests—Autumn & Kelly.

Emotional support and breath mints—Kim and Mom.

It was easy. Not one person said no. I told them what I wished and then stepped aside and let them do it. I have told my kids that to get through life, all you need is one really good friend. Lucky for me, I happen to have lots.

Benjamin's Birthday.

On Saturday, September 22, 2001, I was watching six-year-old Joshua play his game out on the field while trying my best to ignore the soccer warfare taking place inside of me. I was nine months pregnant and just a few days away from the due date of our third-born. I finally surrendered that night and asked a friend to drive me to the hospital to meet Kevin, who was working a night shift in the ER. I was sent upstairs to labor and delivery where they sedated me and my future Pele so we could wait for our soccer coach to get off work. Benjamin was born early the next morning, a Sunday. In the wake of the tragedy twelve days earlier on September 11th, I remember looking down at that baby in my arms and knowing that in a world that had just reached a new level of evil, as long as little babies continued to come, there would always be goodness and hope.

Fast forward ten years. Cancer had entered our home, twice. This time it wasn't leaving without a victim. Knowing that Kevin was nearing the end of his mortal days, I started to panic and prayed that he would please not pass away on Ben's birthday. I was at a point in my life where I prayed to God about everything. I figured that would increase my chances of *some* of my prayers being answered. And I did receive an answer to this prayer, just not the one I expected. God said, "If he does … oh, well." And I knew that was true.

Ben was at the age where Dad could do no wrong. For ten years, they had shared an enthusiasm and love for life, spending hours together with a soccer ball, surf board, or fishing rod. Whenever we had to drive two cars to the same destination, Kevin would announce, "No Hegewald goes alone." (Interpretation: "Who's going to ride with me?") Without fail, Ben was always the first to volunteer. Remembering this, I was at peace. I knew that if Kevin had to pass away on someone's birthday, Ben would probably be the first to volunteer his.

Kevin passed away on September 20th, three days before Benjamin's tenth birthday. We made plans to celebrate Ben's birthday enjoying some Kentucky Fried Chicken at the beach, while watching him ride his new surfboard. With swimsuits on, surfboards loaded, KFC packed, and a houseful of guests ready to join us, out of my mouth escaped the words, "Let's go say hello to your dad—the mortuary is right on the way to the beach."

Silence. Silence and horrified looks. I couldn't believe it myself. I couldn't believe I had the courage to say what my heart had been telling me all day. As we walked out the door, Sam whispered, "I feel so sorry for Ben—it's his birthday."

Earlier that day, I had gone with an adult entourage to visit Kevin at the mortuary. It was a little shocking to see Kevin. I woke up that morning excited, for lack of a better word, to be able to see my husband again, but my brain told me that the person lying in the casket on the table couldn't possibly be him. He was so terribly thin at the end of his life, and the painted lips and eyebrows combined with a comb-over hairstyle were definitely not helping the situation. Fortunately, Rebecca brought her cosmetics and hair clippers and did a little magic, softening makeup and restoring the spiky hairstyle we all knew and loved. We watched with a few giggles as my dad and Kevin's dad and younger brother struggled to get Kevin dressed. It was like watching something out of a movie, although I'm not sure if the genre was comedy or horror. Kevin's upper body kept rising up and down out of the casket as they pulled and tugged his shirt sleeves onto arms unyielding and stiff as a board. Throughout this experience, I kept feeling prompted that I should bring my kids to see Kevin, but each time I would dismiss the thought, due to it being Ben's birthday. I was about to learn an important lesson: don't fight spiritual promptings. Even if you're being told to do something that you might consider cruel and unusual.

As a parent, you can spend your entire life trying to teach your children to believe that God has a plan, and life is precious, and our spirits are immortal. Rarely do you have the chance to prove it. But

I was given that moment. I was reminded again that Someone else knew much better than I what my children needed when I witnessed the shock on each of their faces when they saw their dad. Let's face it: it's scary to see a dead body. It's even more scary to see a dead body if it's your dad—especially if he's wearing make-up. But how grateful I am that my children were able to see their dad privately before being surrounded by friends and guests at the viewing the following morning.

But the moment came after the initial shock wore off, and I was standing with my children surrounding the casket, and they could look down at their dad … and know. The indisputable proof was on the table: the body in front of them was just a body, confirming that the spirit lives, life is to be treasured, and God must have a plan. And it was in that moment that my heart nearly exploded from the raging conflict inside of me. How could this moment of my deepest sorrow also feel like a moment of my greatest blessing? My heart was breaking from the weight of sadness for my children; yet when I looked at them, I thought how they are four of the luckiest children in the world. Now they know.

It took fifteen minutes. That was all the time we spent before we said our goodbyes and headed to the beach. Later, it felt surreal—sitting on the sand, surrounded by so many loved ones who had flown in for the funeral, watching my four children. Josh was far out in the ocean surfing the big waves with dolphins. Sophie and Sam were swimming and doing handstands on the sand. And Ben couldn't stop smiling as he caught wave after wave on his new board. I was grateful that I'd followed the prompting to visit Kevin, and I was more grateful that it hadn't ruined Benjamin's birthday.

Awesome.

Every December I find myself watching *It's a Wonderful Life* while wrapping gifts. I am always struck with a little envy of George Bailey's experience—observing what life would be like if he had never been born. Whenever I think about Kevin's funeral, I classify it as an *It's a Wonderful Life* experience. Although it was Kevin's life being honored, I was the one lucky enough to be left behind to witness the impact he had on so many others. Kevin was friends with everyone. And not just friends—best friends. At least that's the way he made them feel. To walk into a church with over 800 people who in some way had been touched by Kevin was both humbling and empowering. I believe in strength in numbers, and our family was definitely blessed with strength that day. At a time when we should have been weeping, we were buoyed by a higher power and the power of 800 friends who would help absorb our sadness.

Of course, walking into a chapel with all of those people looking at me was a little unnerving. I felt exposed. And I understood now why some widows wear hats with veils covering their faces. My brain felt like it was going to explode from grief and stress and lack of sleep, yet somehow it still knew that I'd look better if I smiled. So as I walked up the long church aisle, with organ music playing and my children surrounding me, I wondered if the spectators thought it was odd to see a widow smiling.

Since I've always had a dramatic flair, I would like to present some awards from the day.

Most Awkward Moment: A funeral director who wouldn't take direction.

The front row of the chapel had been reserved for family. Unfortunately, when we sat down, we couldn't see over the casket. My mom motioned to the funeral director to move the casket to the side. He must have high standards of keeping the casket centered, because they refused. Finally, my brother Matthew jumped up and pushed it to the side himself.

Most Humorous: Van Thompson's pulpit shout-out to the guinea hens.

Kevin and Van's infamous guinea hen episode: what started with twelve, tiny, what-looked-like chicks arriving in the mail grew into a situation involving $700 chicken coops, two very upset wives, a knock on the front door from Animal Control, and twelve, not-so-cute and not-so-small, obnoxiously loud birds being dropped off at the end of the Ortega Highway.

Most Courageous: Josh Hegewald takes the stand.

I was so proud. Josh joined fifty young men—Kevin's "Brothers in Arms"—to sing Kevin's battle cry song, "We'll Bring the World His Truth." If Kevin had been there to vote, I am certain this would have been his favorite part of the show. What's not to love about watching valiant youth singing with all of their hearts while wiping their eyes and noses.

Most Dramatic Moment: Kevin's supposed reincarnation.

There was an audible gasp when Andrew Hegewald, a.k.a. Andylein, Android, Droid, Andreas, Dr. Dre, Drewski, and the latest, Drewski Bobbarewski, began his tribute. The two brothers have a lot of things in common: their looks, mannerisms, unique vocabulary, love for the outdoors, inability to be on time, and—most intriguing at this particular moment—their voices.

Best Actress Award: Me.

And God is deserving of Best Director. I wouldn't change a thing about the funeral service … except who it was for.

After the funeral, we hosted a celebration in our backyard. I say the word "we" as though I had something to do with it. The only thing I had to do was show up. Thanks to a multi-talented team, my yard was transformed with flowers planted in the gardens and tables set with white tablecloths and blue and green table runners and fresh flower arrangements. There were homemade desserts to enjoy and a candy bar with glass canisters filled with Kevin's and my children's favorite sweets. The party atmosphere was complete with balloons, shaved ice, and 100 kids swinging from the treehouse Kevin had built.

At the end of the day, I asked my kids one by one, "How did you feel about today?"

The answer was unanimous: "Awesome." Somehow, beyond explanation, my children were able to participate in their father's funeral and come away thinking the day was awesome. That was spoken after the *first* funeral.

In April 1999, my "therapeutic" running during Kevin's medical residency years earned me a spot on the starting line of the Boston Marathon. I had never seen anything like it—a constant wall of shrieking supporters that continued along the entire 26.2 mile route. I had learned that running long distances requires as much mental strength as it does physical. During long training runs, I had to encourage, persuade, and coerce my legs to continue running when my body was screaming that it wanted to stop. For the Boston Marathon, to motivate me I had arranged for Kevin to be standing at mile seventeen. Amidst the chaos and mass of spectators, Kevin would only be able to see me at this one point before catching me at the finish line. Approaching mile seventeen, I was right on my target time and feeling strong and energetic. Kevin leapt out of the crowd and ran beside me for thirty seconds before sending me off with a rousing, "EYE OF THE TIGER!" I had no idea what he meant by that. I suppose it felt like a *Rocky* moment and I needed to stay focused to make it to the finish line. But by mile twenty, I was approaching the infamous Heartbreak Hill, and I was hitting the wall, which in runner's lingo means: done. Finished. Out of gas. I *walked* up Heartbreak Hill, with people screaming encouragement in my face. But I felt mocked. Twenty years earlier when my dad ran the Boston Marathon, the spectators booed if anyone had the nerve to walk the hill. I think I would have preferred that. I felt like such a loser, I deserved to be treated like one.

Somehow I managed to cross the finish line in just under four hours, a discouraging thirty minutes slower than expected. Kevin missed seeing me. He somehow didn't recognize the broken down mess I had become. He eventually found me an hour later, shivering under an emergency foil blanket, sitting beneath the big "H" for family members to locate their runners. I was so relieved to be rescued.

Planning a second funeral for Kevin in Salt Lake City was like hitting Heartbreak Hill. I was exhausted. My adrenaline long gone.

I came crashing down from the endorphin high that had carried me through the first funeral, and I was done. Instead of having to survive another service, I was ready for someone to hand me a foil blanket so I could go sniffle in the corner.

In a desperate attempt to change the future, I sent a late night email to Stacey: "Stop the presses! Please don't send the SLC funeral program to the printers until you've heard from me." I then looked for a scapegoat on which I could blame the cancellation. I had four children to choose from—I only needed one. I interrogated my kids, searching for one word of apprehension, just one, to escape their mouths. Unfortunately for me, and fortunately for the hundreds of guests who would attend the Salt Lake City funeral, my kids said they were okay with it. They did have one stipulation: they did not want to be tortured by meeting and greeting people before the funeral. Their request was granted. So for an hour and a half before, I stood awkwardly alone in a room in the church hugging people from Kevin's youth—a large number of whom had gray hair and probably wondered why they were still alive when Kevin wasn't.

Much of the funeral service felt like déjà vu. It probably didn't help that I was wearing the exact outfit from the week before. Here I was again, walking down the church aisle with organ music playing and my children around me while parading my freaky smile. The funeral program in Salt Lake was a family affair. We had our moms give prayers, our dads talk, my brother-in-law, Eric, and two of Kevin's best friends, Darin and John (who are like family), give tributes. The only repeat from the San Clemente program was Kevin's brother, Andrew. And since he was in his home territory, no one gasped when they heard his voice like they had at Funeral Number One.

The showstopper was once again the music. Michael, the keyboardist from Kevin's college years rock band, played the guitar while singing "If You Could Hie to Kolob." I told my kids I want that exact number at my funeral so they'd better get going on some guitar lessons. Josh responded, "The guitar is not the problem; we'll have to learn how to sing." The other musical number was twelve of Kevin's closest friends singing an even more obscure song by The Alarm, "Walk Forever By My Side." This was the one song Kevin insisted on using. These same men sang it at Kevin's church mission farewell when they were nineteen years old; it seemed appropriate to have them sing it at his final farewell.

After the service, my father-in-law asked, "Now wasn't that worth it?"

I gave him a resounding, "No!" I hope one day I will be able to change my answer. But I still want to know: what did I get out of my pain and suffering? The only other times I have felt that much pain I was at least handed a baby. Or a medal. Where was my baby? Where was my medal?

U2.

Kevin and I were worlds apart when it came to music. He had an extremely diverse taste in music but felt particularly loyal to '80s rock bands. When all of the CDs from his extensive '80s collection were stolen from his car, he still kept the empty CD cases. I think it was to prove to me that there was someone else out there who recognized the value of a good '80s collection. But there were a few bands we both liked, and at the top of that list was U2.

When Josh wrote an English paper analyzing the lyrics of U2's song, "Sunday, Bloody Sunday," Kevin was so proud he photocopied and mailed (yes, with a stamp) copies of the paper to friends who shared his adoration for Bono. He also created an entire lesson around the song "Pride" on Martin Luther King Day to share with our family. I remember him getting a little emotional during his PowerPoint presentation with the music blaring in the background. And my boys will never forget driving on a dirt road in Idaho, full speed, through a herd of scattering cows with U2's song "Elevation" blasting from the stereo. Suffice it to say, I can't listen to U2 without thinking about Kevin.

We almost didn't check off "Attend a U2 concert" from our bucket list. Kevin gave me U2 concert tickets for a Christmas gift in 2009. Due to Bono hurting his back, the concert was postponed one year to the summer of 2011—the summer in which Kevin was hurting from *his* back being infested with cancer. However, I hold no contempt for Bono. It's not like he was intentionally saying, I will perform "with or without you." But we made it. We celebrated Kevin's forty-third birthday with our good friends Randy and Carri, Kevin's sister Christy, and thousands of middle-aged, pot-smoking U2 die-hards.

Considering Kevin's love for U2, it only seemed appropriate that we play a little U2 during the graveside service. It was actually Kevin's idea to do a pigeon release. His idea, but our responsibility to arrange it. When ten white doves were ordered, I protested that they must be pigeons. I declared that I would gladly take gray pigeons over white doves. I came to find out that all of the times I thought I'd seen white doves released … they were actually pigeons! Doves, once released, will simply fly to the nearest tree to roost, and you will have just purchased, instead of rented, ten doves. Pigeons, however, will continue to fly around until the leader pigeon is released to lead them all home.

I wondered—if pigeons can be perceived as doves, maybe Kevin and I weren't as different as I always judged. I had always considered myself more like a dove—refined, meant to be admired. And Kevin—definitely more like a pigeon. A roamer, living from one moment to the next, searching for discarded food. Yet, it turns out, I'm much more like a pigeon; it's the pigeon, not the dove, who always flies home.

September 30th happened to be an unseasonably warm day in Utah, which made wearing black that much more uncomfortable. Family and close friends gathered at the cemetery, sweating, with nowhere to escape as my little boys ran around with their younger cousins amongst the gravestones. Kevin would be in good company in the Salt Lake Cemetery. My paternal grandparents, TQ Cannon and Kaye Bowman, are buried adjacent to Kevin, with my dear cousin Nate, across the grassy aisle. And of course, I'd be joining him one day. We bought a double-decker plot which means when my time finally comes, I'll be buried on top of him. That seemed right—seeing I was always last to bed.

We all knew that Kevin wouldn't be spending much time hanging around the cemetery. But I'm glad we buried him in Salt Lake City, not only surrounded by mountains, but close to where his parents live. I might have had a hard time sharing Kevin when he was dying, but it's much easier sharing him now that he's dead. This gives them a place where they can come and sit and feel near to him. I have a hundred of those types of places where I live. But I believe that as much as Kevin loved to explore and travel, he had found his favorite place was in our home.

I stood next to Kevin's casket, decorated on top with huge wildflowers, and read to the small crowd excerpts from Kevin's childhood journal about his beloved pigeons. His frustration: "I've lost so many pigeons in my time it's pitiful. I must be the most rotten pigeon fancier in the world." His anticipation: "My pigeon eggs didn't hatch but they look mighty fertile so I still have my hopes for them." And his joy: "I haven't written in a l—o—n—g time but I'll start with my favorite thing—PIGEONS."

Then, with U2's "Beautiful Day" playing, nine white pigeons circled the sky until Sam opened the basket releasing the leader to guide them home. The beauty in this moment is we were all looking up. I don't know where heaven is, but I'm assuming it's somewhere up. So as we were all looking up toward heaven, I imagined Kevin was looking down on us. I told him I loved him. He told me, "I love U2."

Journal.

Sunday, October 2, 2011.

I feel like I'm in a constant battle with Satan—my heart is full of fear. The moment I feel that fear, I try to displace it because I know that fear has no place when faith is present. So I try to rely on my faith—faith that it will all work out. This is the struggle. Because part of me completely and faithfully believes that it will—it will all work out. Yet part of me is dead and is suffering and in that sorrow I can't imagine that it really will all work out. Fear enters in.

First Year Countdown.

What do you do when it's your first morning of being a widow and all of your support staff have returned to their own homes? You get out of bed. That wasn't a riddle. Or a trick question. Just a statement. You get out of bed. You get out of bed today. Then you get out of bed tomorrow. And then you get out of bed the next day. And you do this for the rest of your life. On that first morning, my new initiative began: to survive one year without Kevin.

My mind always seemed to be counting. I counted the number of pages my kids read. I counted how many carbohydrates were in Sophie's brown bag lunch. I counted how many steps it took to walk back from the school and through my front door. I counted how many minutes until I could crawl back into bed, and once there, I counted how many minutes until I had to get up. I counted how many days it had been since Kevin left us. And I counted the number of ways I missed him.

1. I missed him washing the Sunday dinner dishes.
2. I missed having someone who was not afraid to turn on our gas fireplace.
3. I missed buying tomatoes at the grocery store because there was someone in the house who would eat them.
4. I missed his voice.
5. I missed talking to someone who has as much vested interest as I do in our children turning out right.
6. I missed having him take a turn to read with our boys.
7. I missed hearing the television blast at two o'clock in the morning when he was winding down after a late shift.
8. I missed my personal pharmacist, my secret keeper, my friend.

I sensed that an unspoken question by curious outsiders was "What do you do all day?" Friends were concerned and felt the need to fill the empty space. What they didn't realize is that grieving can be a full time job. Grief is not only felt emotionally, but physically as well. The churning stomach, the relentless headache, the constricted chest, the runny nose and leaky eyes all are symptoms of grief. Grief also has this amazing ability to slow down all of one's reflexes and decision-making abilities. When Kevin died, I went from being a highly functioning person, multitasking throughout my day as I handled a household, four children, and a sick husband, to someone whose greatest accomplishment of the day was possibly brushing my teeth. Suddenly I was forced to wonder if that other person ever really existed.

Just because I found the strength to get out of bed each day didn't mean I had enough to venture outside. Three weeks after Kevin passed away, I foolishly accepted an invitation to attend a pressure cooker demonstration at my friend Stacey's house. An hour later I found myself staring out into the rain and unable to get home fast enough. What was my problem? My problem was I found it much too painful to be around friends like Stacey who reminded me of what my life used to be like. There I was at a pressure cooker class thinking, "What the heck is a pressure cooker?" and "Is it my responsibility to make dinner for my family?"

But two days later, I found myself on Stacey's doorstep again. I solicited her help to design some thank you notes. I thought I could handle this because, unlike the pressure cooker class, I was alone and I had actually seen a computer before. As I sat in her workshop, sipping on an oversized cup of pellet ice, I occasionally threw out an opinion as I watched her expertly navigate the computer graphics art world. But I started getting that sinking feeling again when I noticed that she had written my name on my cup with a green marker and had chosen a blue straw, which precisely matched the colors of the Hope for Hegewald graphic on the notecards. It was time to run for the door, and I almost made it without crying when I had to stop and admire her home-sewn Halloween costumes. These encounters were just too painful! I missed my old life—the one where I was capable enough to sew costumes, take computer classes, host a kitchen full of ladies, and quite possibly make dinner for my family using something called a pressure cooker. But interrupting my pity party came the realization that I *never* did those things. The last Halloween costume I made was fourteen years ago when Sophie was two. I sewed sleeves out of a large piece of green felt and called her Peter Pan. And I have no recollection of ever taking a computer class or entertaining with food that came out of a crockpot on steroids. I felt much better about things. I still missed my old life, but at least I stopped comparing it to a life I never led.

Mourning Sickness.

As much as I hated nights, I hated mornings more. Actually, just one painful second in the morning. The moment right before my eyes opened, when a message was sent to my brain trying to make sense of why I was sleeping on Kevin's side of the bed. It didn't matter how many mornings it had been; for that split second, I still couldn't believe that Kevin was really gone. By the time I opened my eyes, my brain, heart, and reality were all aligned once again. And I felt sad. But I am grateful that I had a reason to get out of bed: four incredible children who were probably struggling as much as I was to get up and move forward yet seemed to be doing it so much better than I.

I loved the security daily routines provided. I would spend my mornings making breakfast, packing lunches, reading scriptures, acting happy, and waiting for the moment that I could walk back in the door after walking my boys to school, wearing my pajamas and my fake smile, only to lock the door. I would then busy myself with cleaning up breakfast dishes, reading the obituaries in the newspaper, or playing the piano. It was all an attempt to avoid going upstairs to get dressed. It's not that I minded getting dressed, it's just that then, I was face-to-face with my crying chair.

You see, I had a secret in the closet. Literally—it was in my closet. We have an antique rocking chair that Kevin and I bought when we were living in Virginia. Quite honestly, I think the reputation of North Carolina as creator of the highest quality furniture persuaded us that this chair was, in fact, priceless. As a newlywed homemaker, I bought some fabric and reupholstered it, which entailed cutting the piece of fabric, folding it over the seat, and stapling it on the other side. This chair has earned its pricelessness because I rocked all four of my babies in it. It creaks and the back is too low, but we've stuck with our antique and transported it with our growing family from home to home. Its final resting spot was in our master closet. This rocking chair became my crying chair.

Each morning, as soon as I would kneel near my chair to pray, the tears would begin to flow freely. They quickly elevated to suffocating sobs. This was possibly due to snot interrupting my ability to breath, or vomit coming up from my stomach. Fortunately, my closet is conveniently located next to the bathroom where I would typically end up bent over the toilet. I threw up more times with this "mourning sickness" than I ever did when I was pregnant.

I would shed my share of tears for myself, but most of my tears were for my kids. The weight of my kids' suffering on top of my own was crushing. I could argue that each one of them was at a critical stage in their life as far as needing a dad. Which goes to show that there is no good age to lose a dad.

I'd sob thinking about Josh. He was sixteen, right at the threshold of driving, dating, graduating from high school, and venturing out into the real world. He was definitely forced into foreign territory without his dad. Not only did he inherit the responsibilities of checking the oil in the truck and cleaning the koi pond filters, but I realized the weight he would now bear as the new man of the house. I told Josh he was the luckiest to have had sixteen years of memories with his dad. Josh argued that made the loss that much greater.

I have always felt sorry that Sophie doesn't have a sister, but that hardly compares with not having a dad. And not just any dad, but one that was her personal physician as well. For Sophie's twice a year blood labs, Kevin would sneak into her bedroom before his morning ER shift with all of the necessary supplies to stab her in the arm and fill up a few vials of blood to take to the hospital with him. Sophie definitely didn't sleep through the experience, but nothing could beat the convenience. It was impossible for me not to think about Sophie's future wedding day and her dad not being there without then running for the toilet.

I cried extra tears for Ben. That's because Ben never cries, so I cried for him. I'm smart enough to know that you don't have to shed tears to shed grief; but I also know that grief will continue to grow if it isn't released in some way. Ben lost his best friend the day his dad died, and I felt the most inadequate trying to fill in for Kevin in Ben's life. This is most likely because I can't surf, fish, bike, or play soccer.

And then there was Sam. Sam with his gigantic, sensitive spirit packed inside a little seven-year-old body. Because he had no problem releasing all of the anger, frustration, and sadness inside of him, I probably worried the least about Sam. But he definitely worried the most about me, as evidenced by his asking me two hundred times a day, "Mom, are you okay?" Only once a day, as I tucked him into bed, did he ask, "Mom, am I going to be okay?"

All of that kept me on my knees, sobbing and begging and reminding the Lord of the promise that Kevin was given in a priesthood blessing that our family was going to be okay. Then, an amazing thing would happen. The tears would stop. The Lord is merciful that way. I wiped my eyes, and my nose, and my mouth, and I moved on with my day. I was always blessed with just enough strength to get me through it. I would say farewell to my secret chair, and we both knew I'd be back again tomorrow.

Sam Says the Darnedest Things.

Sunday, October 23, 2011.

I don't know why Sundays are so hard, but they are. The three routine hours we spend in church can be painful, regardless of the emotional turmoil you're suffering. But somehow the smallest things—a line in a hymn, or a phrase by the speaker—can trigger the tears, and I have to just as quickly make them disappear. One Sunday, a few weeks after Kevin died, Sam caught me in one of those moments and asked me why I was sad. I told him I missed Dad. He retorted, "I'm kinda over it." Ah, to be seven years old! I hope Kevin heard Sam's comment. He would have loved it; he probably would have died laughing.

Super Premium.

One of the stark realities of losing a spouse is the weight of feeling like now you're IT—you're all your kids have. This feeling prompted me to invest in life insurance, enough life insurance that my kids won't burden someone else, but not enough that they will be tempted to kill me. Part of the application process included a physical, nothing alarming to be expected. In fact, it was predicted that due to my "good Mormon living" I would most likely achieve "premium status."

When the home visit EMT strapped my arm in the blood pressure cuff, pieces of a conversation I had with my dad about "failing a blood pressure test and needing to take a prescription to help lower it before taking another blood pressure test" flooded my mind. I started to panic. I attempted deep breathing and calm thoughts. The lady looked at me strangely. Trying not to break into a sweat, I asked her if anything was the matter. She said, "Is your blood pressure usually this low?" I didn't have the heart or the desire to tell her that my heart had recently been broken, and I was actually quite relieved with the news that it was still, in fact, beating. However slowly. Well, my slow beating heart and my good Mormon living earned me not "premium" status, but "SUPER premium" status! I didn't even know there was such a thing. Here are a few of my super premium secrets.

I DO NOT:

1. Drink alcohol
2. Smoke, chew, or like the smell of tobacco
3. Use, nor ever did use, any of Kevin's fentanyl lollipops
4. Drink caffeine, unless it's diet and served over pellet ice
5. Exercise, except walking my kids to school in my pajamas

6. Go to bed without first having a bowl of ice cream

7. Stand in front of the microwave

8. Snore (Kevin is not here to dispute this)

9. Text and drive

So now I'm the proud owner of a life insurance policy that I hope to never use. And because of this experience, I can look in the mirror, past the grief-stricken, wrinkled mess that is staring back at me, and try to think about how I look from the inside … and I look rather SUPER premium.

Kindness Among Death and Taxes.

Shortly after Kevin's death, I met with our accountant. He made the comment, "You know, if this situation was reversed, Kevin would be much worse off than you are." It's true. Kevin and I had a pretty fabulous arrangement: he earned all the money, and I managed it. (I prefer the word "managed" to "spent.") I was the keeper of all expenses, bills, bank statements, and passwords. Except for one. One day before Kevin passed away, as I was trying to log in to our bank account, the bank didn't recognize the computer. It asked the security question: When is your wedding anniversary? Easy! I typed in June 23, 1992, and was rewarded with a "that is incorrect." Huh? I then realized that was Kevin's security question … which meant I was in trouble! I tried June 24, June 22; I tried 1991, 1993; and every possible derivative of our actual wedding anniversary.

I finally hollered at Kevin for help: "When is our wedding anniversary?!"

His response: "June."

Bingo!

I relied on the help of our accountant to set up an appointment with the Social Security office to discuss death benefits for the kids and me. He even willingly tagged along for support. When we entered a building full of hearing-aided folks, I was again reminded that forty-three is much too young to be a widow. The advantage, however, was the receptionist recognized me as a person who would be able to answer all of the questions without asking to have them repeated, and I was escorted to a case worker immediately. This appointment was to be the first of five, but after just one hour of answering questions with my case-worker, Annette, she excused me with the news that she would take it from there and didn't need me to return. Never take for granted properly functioning ears. Annette not only sent me out the door with her direct number but with the official death certificate I had been required to provide.

She kindly commented, "I know those certificates cost money so I will just make a copy of it." Yes, they do cost money. And the mortuary advised me to order at least twelve of them. Guess how many I have used? Two. I sent one to Kevin's life insurance company and the other to his employer. Other than that, everyone else just seems to take my word for it. I assume as soon as they hear me explain in my youthful sounding voice that my husband has passed away from cancer, they pretty much believe me. Not one person has challenged me with a "prove it." So I left the Social Security office that day thankful for my hearing, thankful I had a hardworking husband, and thankful that there are people like Annette in the world.

Hegewalds Can Do Hard Things.

Hard, Harder, Hardest. Those are three words I have redefined. Something that used to be described as "THE hardest" is now tucked away under just hard. When our kids were young, our family rotated and recycled through several family mottos. But no motto prepared us more for our eventual trial than "Hegewalds can do hard things." Sufficient to say, the year Kevin passed away we faced a lot of hard things. Even the hard things could be differentiated into either "lump in the throat hard" or "punch in the gut hard."

Seeing only my name on the third grade class list.

Filling out a form only to discover none of the words "single" "married" or "divorced" accurately describe me. (I checked married, only having to delete it later when it required my spouse's information.)

Cashing a life insurance check.

Having to call a doctor to set up a real appointment in an actual doctor's office.

Reading Sam's journal entry: "I have five people in my family."

When a local newspaper columnist wanted to feature our family in an article about doing hard things, it opened up the topic for us. Passing out little slips of paper, I asked the kids to write down one hard thing they have had to do. They all looked at me as though I had just grown a second head. Sophie replied with a little sarcasm, "Um, don't you think we'll all write the same thing?" Not surprisingly, they did … somewhat.

Sam: Losing my dad and waking up in the morning. (He loves his sleep.)

Ben: Going to my daddy's ceremony. (Ceremony = funeral. I knew those funerals were harder than they let on!)

Sophie: Watching Dad suffer.

Josh: Dealing with Dad dying.

Apparently, the experience of losing someone they loved was hard, but watching him suffer was harder. This couldn't be better illustrated than by an interaction I had with Josh one day a few months after Kevin's death. When I shared the sad news that our neighbor's brother-in-law had died suddenly and unexpectedly from a heart attack, Josh's response was, "Lucky." WHAT?! I launched into a convincing one-sided debate as to how fortunate we were to have had six months to prepare for our dad's death. Financial, spiritual, and emotional matters were all in perfect standing order, and final "I love yous" had been shared before Kevin passed away. Josh sat and listened to his overly zealous mother until I finally conceded the debate floor to him.

Josh countered with, "He didn't have to suffer."

Oh.

In a future session with my psychologist, he guided me through my error of trying to convince someone of my own convictions rather than just validating the way they feel. That's one of the hardest things—being told that you've done something wrong.

Oops, change of words: not hardest, just hard.

The Hardest.
Journal. September 28, 2011.

1. *Putting his toothbrush away in a drawer.*
2. *Seeing his running shoes and Vans by the front door.*
3. *Opening the drawer for my car keys and seeing his wallet.*
4. *Making a phone call from my car and hearing "Kevin" said by the car computer.*
5. *Seeing only five piles of laundry in the hall.*
6. *Sleeping on his side of the bed.*
7. *Asking for his t-shirt from the mortuary, only to be handed a shirt cut in pieces.*
8. *Reading his journal.*
9. *Planning a second funeral.*
10. *Saying prayers with the children and not being able to say "please bless Daddy."*
11. *Going to bed at night.*
12. *Waking up in the morning.*

TableTopics.

Thank goodness for the invention of *TableTopics*. Packed inside a little clear box are one hundred thirty-five questions that are designed to spark a conversation around the dinner table. We found that they were especially helpful in distracting us from noticing the empty seat at the table, as well as forcing us to talk about something other than what we were all thinking.

TableTopic: Do you have any of the physical traits seen in your family?
Mom: You all have Dad's mouth and smile. And you all have big noses thanks to your Smith ancestors.
All (except Josh): We don't have big noses! Just Josh! Where did we get our blonde hair from?
Mom: What do you mean? Both Dad and I have blonde hair.
Kids: HUH??
I had to clarify that we both were born with blonde hair, and then Kevin went bald, and I went chemically blonde. Details.

TableTopic: Would you rather be spanked or grounded?
Josh: It depends who is doing it. Mom—spanked. Dad—grounded.
Everyone laughs.
Sam: Remember when me and Ben were playing the Toy Story game and Josh was babysitting and we woke up Dad and …
Josh: … he about took off my head! (With a German *Backpfeife*, or slap on the head.)
Ben: We lost electronics for a week!
Josh: Electronics?! I about lost my head!!!
It kind of felt good to verbalize a not-so-wonderful memory of Kevin. Let's face it—Kevin was becoming immortalized. But my children said it like "It is what it is." I'm glad they felt like they could say it.

TableTopic: What is the saddest event you have dealt with?
Sophie: That's a little obvious. Skip.

TableTopic: Would you rather be an only child or have 10 siblings?
Every one of them: 10 siblings!

See, they do love each other! Even when they don't show it.

I'm Right Here.

An odd phenomenon happens when someone dies: the junk they leave behind quickly becomes priceless. One day the piles of paper and clutter of clothes are an annoyance, and the very next day those same items have magically transformed into endearments. I have wondered if it would be easier to sort through a house full of belongings of someone who passed away at ninety-nine, or live in a house that looks like we are expecting our deceased to walk back in the door tomorrow. The medicine on the bathroom counter, the scriptures on the nightstand, the shoes lined up in the closet, each perfectly in place yet out of place as they patiently await the return of their owner. It's ironic the attachment I felt to Kevin's things; they have no worth or value other than that they belong to Kevin—or did.

I had a charitable intention after Kevin's funeral that left as quickly as it came. As a thank you, I considered giving each of the men who participated in the program one of Kevin's ties. I took all of Kevin's ties and arranged them on the floor of our walk-in closet. Having a job that didn't require a tie, Kevin's collection was by no means exorbitant. But each one of his ties was entwined with memories—weddings, Father's Day gifts, missionary service, Sunday meetings. Looking at his ties, my heartstrings snapped, and I spent the next fifteen minutes crying while hanging them all back up, knowing that I wouldn't be able to part with a single one.

The room in our house where I could be buried alive in all of Kevin's junk was his home office, which is overstuffed with furniture and books and frames on the wall. After he died, it became my playground. When the kids were at school or late at night when I should have been sleeping, I felt like an archaeologist, digging through journal articles, paper piles, and yellow legal pads filled with scrawled notes, searching for clues of Kevin's last intentions, motivations, or his thoughts. I studied the papers wondering if Kevin found this particular article interesting, or if he ever called this certain phone number scribbled on a scrap, and if he did, what was discussed. I cracked open his briefcase, now confined to the corner and covered with dust since it was no longer being transported to church. Packed inside were all of his church essentials: youth manuals, more yellow legal pads of paper, a half empty tin of Altoids, a pack of bubble gum, a half dozen pens and pencils, a few highlighters. I removed nothing. I clicked it closed and returned it to its corner. I became buried in grief as my search uncovered mounds of unfinished projects and unfulfilled dreams. In all of my searching, I couldn't help but dream of finding a little hidden note written to me. Something simple. Probably scribbled on a little scrap of yellow lined paper. Perhaps just a "Hi, Abby. I hope you know I think you're doing a great job. Love, Kevin."

No note for me yet. But several for my kids. Kevin ambitiously wanted to write letters to each of our children before he died which they could open on the significant milestones that he would miss. Unable to type or write with hands that no longer functioned, the task was to be accomplished by Kevin speaking into a digital recorder. However, the greatest difficulty proved to be finding the time—time without friends or family wanting to visit and time not in a drug-induced coma. I was concerned. This was one project I wouldn't be able to complete if left undone, along with recording his personal history, which apparently was never a priority to Kevin. I warned him that it wasn't such a good idea leaving his mom and me to write his life story because we would probably argue about the details.

He simply replied, "That's okay; there are so many interpretations to one's life anyway."

I did my best to support Kevin in his desire to accomplish the letters as we felt his time to go drawing near. A "No visitors please" sign was attached to the front door—much to Kevin's dismay and my relief. If I had been the one diagnosed with cancer, I would have returned home from the doctor, slapped that sign on the door immediately, and hunkered down with my family until they put me into the ground. As for the drug-induced comas, I just prayed like crazy that when Kevin was talking into the recorder his words would make sense. This was a legitimate concern. One night when Kevin still had the ability to text, he started off on the right train of thought to a good friend and coworker, but somehow ended with "I love you sweetheart." Of course, that was better than the next night's text that said, "what dacchh kan i zayyyy yiuknow man?" It was probably a good idea that he chose my sister to be in charge of transcribing the letters and sending them to our children at the appropriate times because, unlike me, she wouldn't be tempted to edit them.

Sam was the first to receive a letter from his dad. Six weeks after Kevin passed away, Sam turned eight years old and was baptized. Josh had just received the proper priesthood authority in our church, so he willingly, but nervously, accepted the responsibility to baptize his younger brother. I am so grateful that he could take the place of his dad to perform this special ordinance. Mercifully, the anxiety Josh felt immediately dispersed when he felt the presence of his dad. Kevin was probably late. I mean, let's face it, we presumably take our personalities and habits with us to the next life. But this was an event he wouldn't miss. Expecting to only feel joy at this happy occasion, I instead was consumed with the most intense sorrow that Kevin wasn't sitting next to me. Looking back, he probably was. There are likely many times when Kevin is standing right beside me, wanting to shake me and shout, "Abby, I'm right here!!"

One night, he definitely got my attention.

Our master bedroom is in the corner on the second story of our house, facing the backyard. Kevin developed the delightful habit of blasting our bedroom window with hose water whenever he was locked out of the house after a late night shift. When I heard the indistinguishable noise, my eyes would fly open and my brain would race to interpret the sound of water pounding on the window. I'd slip out of bed, lift the blinds, and see Kevin in his work scrubs holding the garden hose.

After Kevin passed, each night when I was getting ready for bed, I would be struck with the familiar sound of water hitting the window. I dismissed it, crediting the sound to rain or the sprinklers. But too many dry mornings, and randomly late bedtimes, soon left me perplexed as to the source of the spraying water. Night after night, I was greeted by the mystifying sound. Finally I consigned myself to the fact that Kevin was trying to get my attention. With the sound of water hitting the glass, I crawled up onto the window sill, pulled my knees up, and looked out into the empty, dark night. I finally allowed the flood gates to open and the reservoir of tears to be released. My heart ached and longed for that moment of lifting the blinds and seeing Kevin in his scrubs with the garden hose. But I still got the message. My husband was shouting, "Abby, I'm right here!"

Journal.
Friday, November 18, 2011.

Michael, my personal Apple computer consultant, who is really just my friend, came over last night to help me with some computer issues. Four hours later ...

The situation reminded me so much of working with Kevin. I would state the problem: "My dock has disappeared from my homepage." Then the search would begin, and while fixing that problem, "Let's restart the router so the internet is faster" and "Let's put these controls on so ..." It would make me want to yell, "All I wanted you to do is find my dock!" (yelling at Kevin, not Michael). But last night I needed Michael's help with Kevin's iPhone. I haven't known what to do with it. I have already visited the AT&T store three times, each time with the intent to either turn it off or make it Sophie's. And each time I've left emotionally unable to do either. Michael and his genius skills helped transfer all of Kevin's iPhone information onto the computer. Oh my. We stored his contacts, his texts (which were encoded; darn, I would like to have read them), photos taken on his phone, and, most importantly, the recordings of the blessings Kevin gave the children before their first day of school. As we were searching the phone, we found a treasure—a little blip of Kevin singing "Lead Kindly Light." It was terrible singing ... and I loved it! Michael said, "Now, that's worth keeping. If someone just says 'testing 1,2,3,' you delete it. But if they sing, it's a keeper." I can't believe I could keep myself from crying when I heard Kevin's voice. It's probably because it really was that bad, and that made me smile.

Photos.

For some unknown reason, I love torturing myself by looking at photos of Kevin on family outings. There is something strangely satisfying about logging in to iPhoto and having my heart ripped open. I feel like I am diving into a deep pool full of wonderful memories to swim around in. And as long as I remember to come up for air every so often, I avoid drowning in the thought that this is as large as this reservoir of memories with Kevin will ever be.

Losing a loved one makes you want to take more pictures every day. And it makes you want to invest in the added warranty or security package on every storage device you will ever buy in the future. On Christmas Eve, 2010, I was worried when I discovered that our digital camcorder was full. Kevin was given the task of downloading it to the computer so we would have space to capture the magic of Christmas. The following morning as we were filming happy Christmas moments, our computer hard drive was in the process of crashing, melting, and falling into oblivion. It's been said you can't put a price on a picture. I can. I know exactly what price we paid to have our photos recovered. $1400. And we willingly paid it because those pictures were proof of a lifetime of experiences.

When our new hard drive was returned four months later with the recovered photos on it, our life was chaotic as Kevin had just been diagnosed. All I had time for was a quick peek to see that there were over 11,000 photos. It wasn't until several months later that I discovered that 8,000 of those photos were in fact duplicates, and three entire years of our digital lives were missing. Despite knowing what true devastation feels like, I still felt devastated. But it's amazing the perspective that comes from dealing with cancer, and soon I stopped mourning the photos I no longer had and started rejoicing in the ones I did.

I've memorized every one of the 3,269 photos in my iPhoto library. For months after Kevin passed away I would spend hours and hours foraging, hoping to find just one overlooked photo of Kevin. Searching through these photos, I was faced with a stark reality: Kevin will forever be frozen in time as an active, young, forty-three-year-old man. Only I will grow old and decrepit. Where is the justice in that? And I've even lost the one person who would still tell me I'm beautiful, all wrinkled and gray. I often imagine a scene forty years from now, how delusional I will look when I show off a picture of the handsome young man I am married to.

With a renewed love and appreciation for pictures, we invited a photographer to both funerals. I don't know if this is normal. I didn't ask. But I love that I have pictures I can refer to that captured the details that were overlooked in my despondent state of mind. I am grateful for photos documenting the incredible displays of Kevin's life in our San Clemente church foyer. It took talent, time, and a ten-foot truck to transport family portraits, quilts, Kevin's bike, surfboard, soccer cleats, medical lab coat, guitar, and everything else not nailed down in our home. One minute of standing in that foyer reminded everyone that Kevin had lived life to its fullest, inspiring them to get out there and do the same.

When I look at these photos now, I love the pictures of the amazing flowers on top of Kevin's casket. The enormous spray of white roses, lilies, white berries, and green pine displayed at the San Clemente service was breathtaking. In contrast, the casket in Salt Lake City was decorated with huge yellow sunflowers and colorful wildflowers, representing Kevin's bright personality and the return to his beloved mountains.

I especially love any pictures of my children, smiling or laughing with their cousins or friends. I couldn't feel more comfort than when I look at the pictures of the five of us, arms around one another, standing next to the casket in both San Clemente and Salt Lake City, smiling.

A friend of Sophie's posed the question, "How can you smile at a time like this?"

Sophie's response: "Because my dad would want us to."

But in the hundreds of pictures that were taken, there are two I love the most. The first one is of Sam looking at his dad in the casket. Seven-year-old Samuel, all handsome in his dark blue suit jacket, sporting a white rose boutonniere, his little hands both gently resting on the side of the casket. You can catch a glimpse of a blue and green Hope for Hegewald band on his wrist. But it's his face; his sweet little freckled face has the most serene, peaceful look. And maybe a hint of curiosity. Innocent Sam had the ability to stroke Kevin's face and arms and hands as he was passing away, leading him to make the remarkable observation that his skin was growing whiter and colder. This curiosity would lead to future questions like, "Is Dad's body a skeleton yet?" or "I wonder if Dad is a fossil." (These questions did coincide with a science unit on rocks and fossils in school.) This fascination with the human body made me wonder if Sam would follow in his dad's medical footsteps; that is, if he chooses to forgo his plans of making it big in Hollywood. So I see that hint of curiosity in the picture. But the predominant emotion on Sam's face is peace. I've framed this shot of Sam and his dad. To me, it captures all that is lovely and good and all that can be learned and endured from a heart-breaking experience. Time will tell how much of Sam's future therapy will be spent ruminating on the fact that his mother displayed a picture in their home of him looking at his deceased father.

The other picture I love is of me, and it is by definition the worst picture ever taken of me. If my photographer friend in Salt Lake City had taken time to edit the pictures, he would have considered it a favor to destroy its very existence and the future possibility of it being circulated on the internet. I'm so glad he didn't. I had just endured an hour-and-a-half of awkwardly hugging friends, relatives, and people I'd never met before. A family prayer was about to be said before entering into the chapel of the church for the funeral service. It was the only time no eyes were on me … except the eye of the photographer. I had let my guard down. The smile was gone. And with that, my face drooped and sagged, and my eyes sunk into their dark sockets. A few too many years had been added to my face, though I still looked far too young to be a widow. The only two redeeming qualities of the photo are my hair—which looked fabulous thanks to Rebecca, who followed me to Salt Lake City—and my cheekbones—which looked striking due to the gauntness of my face. But these two graces cannot atone for my overall appearance of sorrow, misery, sadness, distress, heartache, agony, torment, woe, or any other word in the thesaurus under "how I feel." And that's why I love it. It is the only one of the 438 photos where my exterior gives the slightest glimpse into how my heart was broken on the inside. I have this picture hanging in my closet, right next to my crying chair. I stare at it every day. It's like looking at a picture of my soul.

My iPhoto library continues to grow, just as my children do. Birthdays and holidays, music programs and school award assemblies, sports games and tennis matches, first days of school and high school formals, beach outings and family vacations—each picture living proof that time marches on.

I was proven wrong about one thing. I used to drown in the thought that Kevin would no longer be a part of our growing collage. But that's not true; he makes appearances. Riding a hot air balloon and basking in a sunset at the beach on the one-year anniversary of his passing. Standing in two feet of snow at Christmas while delivering an evergreen wreath to his grave. Holding a bottle of his favorite hot sauce in a little hole-in-the-wall in Washington, D.C. Yes, Kevin's face isn't captured, but he is still very much a part of my growing photo library.

Sam Says the Darnedest Things.
Monday, November 28, 2011.

As Sam and I were snuggling in his bed, we started talking about Kevin and the possibility of a "rewind" in heaven—being able to ask God if you can rewind and watch a particular scene from your life. Our scenes of interest always involve something that was lost and never found, such as the case of Joshua's lost school binder, or Kevin's lost iPhone, or the mysterious disappearance of Sam's special baby blanket Sophie sewed for him. One day, Sam wondered aloud if Dad had already asked about his phone. I told him that maybe dad wasn't concerned about it anymore. Sam looked at me very seriously and said, "Oh, I am for sure asking about my blanket."

Abby Normal.

I am finally living up to one of my nicknames. It comes from the classic movie *Young Frankenstein.* There is a scene in which Dr. Frankenstein, played by Gene Wilder, puts a brain into this eight-foot monster he has created. The monster flips out and goes all crazy and psychotic before the doctor sedates him. He then asks his assistant, Igor (now this is really only funny if you can hear it in Gene Wilder's voice with the appropriate dramatic pauses):

Dr: Do you mind telling me whose brain I put in?

Igor: And you will not be angry?

Dr: I will NOT … be angry.

Igor: Abby someone.

Dr: Abby someone. Abby who?

Igor: Abby normal.

I was okay with being called "Abby Normal" because quite honestly I've never felt abnormal. Until now. As strong as this cancer experience has made me in some ways, my heart has grown more fragile. I know that a normal person would not typically cry while listening to Kermit the Frog and Miss Piggy singing "Rainbow Connection." Nor would they be so disturbed and unable to sleep when a main character on *Downton Abbey* is killed. I might be the only person on earth with no desire to see *The Hunger Games.* I read the books and loved them, but that was pre-Cancer Round Two, and now the thoughts of watching children try to kill other children is horrifying. I recognize the abnormal behavior of ordering a pizza once a week just so I can see the name "Kevin" written on the side of the box or calling Josh's cell phone twice a day just to hear Kevin's voice leave the greeting: "This is Joshua Hegewald's personal secretary. Please leave your name and matter of business at the sound of the beep and I will try to get back to you. Thank you, and have a good day." I also realize that a normal person might not stand perfectly still while watering the garden, watching a hummingbird flit in and out of its hose water bath. Of course, I learned that from Kevin. He wasn't normal either, even before cancer.

Cancer changes a person—the survivor, too, as they are left to reflect on all the victim has embodied. I am definitely more perceptive of nature now. It makes me feel closer to Kevin. Every time I see a vibrant sunset, or interesting cloud shapes, I imagine Kevin having a small part in creating those specifically for me. And watching an ordinary pigeon walk through our backyard is like reading a love letter from him.

I used to ridicule Kevin for returning home from interesting or exotic places with a camera roll of pictures strictly of the outdoor surroundings. In the hundreds of pictures from his ten-day trip to Guatemala and Belize with Joshua and Sophie, there is only one—ONE!—picture of just the three of them together. And I can't say that I love it. In an attempt to scare his older brother while snorkeling in Belize, Kevin stealthily swam up from behind to grab him, but instead rammed the top of his head into a piece of coral. He was bleeding profusely, so the diving guides pulled Kevin out of the water and into the boat and then watched as the "ER doc" attempted to patch himself up. With limited supplies, Kevin cleaned the wound before wrapping an entire roll of gauze tape around his head—"around" as in over the head and under his chin. He looked like a head injury victim during the Civil War. And that's the picture: Joshua and Sophie smiling on each side of the wrapped up man I had entrusted them to in a foreign country.

Maybe I shouldn't complain; at least this picture was proof that they were there. Unlike when Kevin returned home from interviewing for medical school at George Washington University in Washington, D.C., with only four pictures of the "biggest squirrels" he'd ever seen. I kindly offered my photography expertise that perhaps he should have included one of the national monuments in the background so people could actually see that the "biggest squirrels" were in fact in Washington, D.C.

Of course, Kevin had a soft spot for squirrels. One summer, after discovering that baby squirrels were tunneling beneath the storage shed in our backyard, Kevin made the humane decision to live-trap them instead of listening to my less-humane suggestion of using poison to get rid of them. Kevin successfully trapped four baby squirrels and put the trap in the back of our car for the drive to church. He stopped at a grassy, weedy spot and proceeded to release the lucky little varmints to their freedom. Unfortunately, at the last second, one of the squirrels redirected his course and instead of running up the hill ran into the road … right as Kevin accelerated the car. The thump was undeniable, and the kids looked out the back window at the small lump in the middle of the road.

Kevin hollered out, "It's just stunned. It's not dead." (He would have made a wonderful veterinarian.)

We took a different route home from church that afternoon.

I can't say cancer has changed me into an animal lover. But I might pause a little longer than normal whenever I see a flock of birds or a furry little animal … even if it's lying in the road.

Journal.
Friday, December 2, 2011.

The wind finally stopped after two days of howling. I swept the front porch and netted the leaves out of the spa and the koi pond. I love working outside (except when it's cold). Every morning when I wake up and go into our bathroom, I see the trees outside my window—all green, except one. I don't know the name of it. Kevin always knew the names of everything in our garden. But this tree is a special one because Kevin planted it. And the leaves right now are a magnificent bright yellow, the only vibrant color against the white stone wall. The first time I noticed it, I immediately thought, "Oh, I wish Kevin could see this!" And then I realized he probably does. He's probably even more amazed that I noticed it, too.

Christmas.

One of the first lines I penned after Kevin passed away was "I am worried about my own mortality, and I am worried about Christmas." Three months away and one of my very first thoughts was *How am I going to survive Christmas?* That is, if I'm still alive. I made a decision: we would be going to Salt Lake City for the holiday, a first in fifteen years. A 700 mile trip, all to avoid a thirty-second moment.

I read a study that stated that one common factor that the "happiest families" share is that they celebrate family traditions. I'm guessing they interviewed my happy parents somewhere in there, because my childhood memories of Christmas are deeply embedded in tradition. Christmas Eve menu of ham rolls, green and red jello, and Granny's sour cream cookies. Performing talents and reenacting the Nativity. Singing "The Twelve Days of Christmas" with Aunt Jane vibratoing as the "seeevvenn swaaaannss a swwimmmminggg" and my granddad as the partridge in a pear tree. Christmas morning consisted of marching down the stairs youngest to oldest, burying ourselves in wrappings, and filling our bellies with my mom's sausage soufflé and homemade eggnog.

Marrying into the Hegewald family, I was introduced to a traditional German Christmas, which is celebrated on December 24th. The night includes ham and cheese Brötchen, reading the Nativity story, and singing "Stille Nacht" around the piano. It also seems to involve a lot of fire—a roaring fire in the fireplace, at least a dozen lit candles spinning the propellers on German Nativity pyramids, and always the burning of some headache-inducing incense. The serenity of the evening is interrupted by a knock on the door and a "Ho, ho, ho" by someone who claims to be Santa but who looks more like a neighbor with a gray beard wearing a red robe. All presents are distributed and opened, followed by a round of hot Pero and plates of German S*tollen.*

Once Kevin and I moved to California with little Josh and Sophie, we decided that we would spend Christmas morning in our own home before making the trek to Salt Lake City to see our parents. Kevin and I were both excited to continue and create our own traditions. Christmas Eve found us celebrating in different homes with various friends each year, but the tradition of acting out the Nativity continued. Our culminating event, however, was not someone wearing a red robe, but Kevin usually putting on his white lab coat and heading to the ER. Working on Christmas Eve was the price we had to pay for having New Year's Eve off while we were in Utah. So I'd be left alone on Christmas Eve to put out cookies and milk for Santa, wrestle restless kids to bed, and set the stage for the magic of Christmas morning.

Hearing the door unlock at 7:30 a.m. the next morning could never come early enough for the four kids waiting anxiously in my bed. The sound of Dad home from work signaled that Christmas morning could finally begin. Kevin had adopted my dad's tradition of being the first person to enter the family room—to turn on the Christmas tree lights, "ohh" and "ahh" over all of the sights that had filled our kids' dreams, and then to turn on the video camera to capture that magical moment of happy children running down the stairs.

It was that moment, that thirty-second moment, of turning on the lights and calling for the kids, that I traveled 700 miles to avoid. Surprisingly, by the time December rolled around, I had faced so many hard things that I knew I had the courage to also face that moment. But I'm glad I didn't have to. It was the right decision to go to Utah. If anything, I needed to surround myself with people who loved and missed Kevin as much as we did. My children were forgiving of the broken traditions—well, all except Sam.

It all started with a donated Christmas tree. Well, not really; it actually all started with four mysterious pumpkins dropped off at our front door the week before Halloween. The outpouring of love and support that began when Kevin was diagnosed continued long after Kevin had left us. The only difference was that gifts once received on the doorstep from the arms of a friend were now left anonymously with no one to thank or to hug. Those four pumpkins, meant to save me from having to venture out into the real world, were seen as an insult to Sam who now couldn't go to the pumpkin patch to pick out his own pumpkin. (Side note: I take my kids to Walmart to choose their pumpkins; this pumpkin patch idea is an ongoing dream of Sam's.) Recalling Sam's reaction to the pumpkins, I couldn't imagine how he was going to react to the news that friends were picking up, purchasing, and setting up a Christmas tree for our home. Sam declared, "First they ruined Halloween, now they're ruining Christmas! What's next? A basket full of eggs that have already been colored?!"

Picking out the Christmas tree is one of our favorite family traditions. We drive a mile and a half to the Lowe's parking lot, and where others see only a lot full of trees, my kids see a virtual playground for a wicked game of hide-and-go-seek. As I set to task searching for the perfect seven-foot Noble, the kids scatter looking for the perfect hiding spot. That game has provided many good laughs when an unsuspecting buyer lifts up a tree only to discover a child hiding in the dark behind it.

I never take as long as my children wish I would to decide on a tree. After I'd make my selection, Kevin would load it up in the back of his truck and we'd make the short journey home, anticipating the first batch of homemade eggnog.

Of course the tradition wouldn't be complete without Kevin yelling at the kids to help "open that door" or "spread out that sheet of plastic," and me saying, "a little more to the left, to the left, to the left, to the right now" until the tree was perfectly straight. And then all five of them would head off to bed, leaving behind a sink full of empty Christmas mugs to wash and a box of lights to be strung.

I couldn't imagine going to the Christmas tree lot without Kevin. I thought the problem would be solved if we didn't get a tree, since we wouldn't be at home to celebrate Christmas morning anyway. But our friends insisted and set up a perfectly straight, seven-foot Noble in the corner of our family room. I knew it was purchased from off the back of a truck for a school fundraiser, and it was better that way—

Sam wouldn't like the thought of some other family playing their own game of hide-and-go-seek searching for our tree. And the tree looked lovely filling the space that, if left empty, would have been a constant reminder why this Christmas was definitely not like the last. Not that we needed reminding.

Unfortunately, the Christmas tree drama followed us to Utah. My mother put Sam in charge of Christmas morning. She had learned, as I had, that our family's happiness centered around our eight-year-old's happiness. The big decisions were up to him: where everyone would sleep, whether we would walk downstairs and celebrate next to the tree in the basement, or if we would walk upstairs and celebrate on the main floor of the house. Once Sam had processed the layout of GG and Granddad's house and pictured how the tree would sit in their living room amid the grand piano, fireplace and red velvet sofas, he was horrified to hear that the ten-foot Christmas tree was actually in the entryway, not the living room. Bending over backwards to appease my power-wielding child, my parents lovingly took ten minutes to move the tree from the entry way into the living room and then spent the next three hours putting it all back together when it came crashing down just moments later, breaking limbs and ornaments. But by the time we arrived the next day, the tree was magnificently standing next to the fireplace, right where Sam wanted it.

One of the first things I do when I enter my mom's kitchen is search out her "meltaway" cookies. They are usually hidden in her freezer, or outside in her garage, which in the Utah winter is as cold as her freezer. They are never too difficult to find because my mom bakes hundreds of these cookies at Christmas time. Each melt-in-your-mouth cookie has her distinctive touch of swirled green or pink frosting. My mother has taken this signature meltaway cookie to her annual Christmas cookie party with ten of her girlfriends every single year for the past thirty-five years. She has always claimed that they would kick her out if she didn't provide her standard nine dozen—each plate tied up merrily in cellophane and red ribbon. But for some reason, this year, the Survive First Christmas Without Kevin year, she made Greek baklava. After thirty-five years. I was dumbfounded. And disappointed. The only explanation I could come up with was maybe she was looking for a reason to be kicked out of the group. But they didn't kick her out, and she reported that they even liked her homemade baklava.

Each time I opened her freezer door for a meltaway that wasn't there, I was reminded how disappointing life can be. But part of me knows my mom well enough to conclude that maybe she wanted to show her daughter that even the best, long-standing traditions don't last forever. And it's never too late to start new ones.

New Year's Goals.

Yep, every January, we make resolutions in the Hegewald household. After the year of Kevin's sickness and death, we desperately hoped that the next year would be better than the last. (There's no way it couldn't be, right?) Benjamin was in charge of our goal-setting family activity, so he made a little worksheet for everyone to document their ambitions. I chimed in with the exact same speech I deliver every year—the importance of goal-setting, how we should always strive to be improving ourselves, my strong belief that if you write something down you increase your chance of it actually happening. I think my kids probably heard, "Blah, blah, blah."

So I felt a little guilty about leaving my worksheet blank. Under the guise that I would help Sam now, and do mine later, it glared at me for the next few weeks—begging, prodding. I had become a little cynical about goal setting after the past year. I couldn't remember what goals I set the previous January, but it's pretty safe to say I accomplished none of them. Looking back, I realized I had achieved quite a few accomplishments that year that weren't preemptively plotted. If I had owned a crystal ball in the January before Kevin passed, I imagine my goal worksheet might have looked like this:

Spiritual goals:
Develop a deep relationship with my Savior by striving to better understand and appreciate His Atonement for me.
Solidify my testimony that God has a plan and that faith and hope are essential, but it only works if my desires are aligned with the Lord's.
Live knowing that families can be together forever.

New talent:
Start a blog. Discover the healing power of writing about something that you think will destroy you. Be the proud owner of a seventy-six

page hardback blog-turned-book with my name on it.

Social goal:
Plan a funeral. Make decisions concerning burial arrangements, a casket, an obituary, and a program, and have the good sense to delegate all other details.
Do this twice.

Educational goals:
Meet many new, interesting friends and learn something from each of them.
From oncologists, learn that someone else always has it worse than you.
From hospice nurses, that compassion is one of the most Christ-like attributes.
From mortuary directors, communication would be better if all of their clients were dead.
From social security workers, time really is irrelevant to the government.
And from personal finance advisors, that against popular belief, money markets really don't work as hard as I do.

Physical goal:
Survive. Even when the person you love most doesn't.

I know those weren't the goals I wrote down, but that was my life. Which leads me to the conclusion that life is what happens when you set off to accomplish one thing and end up achieving something else.

So what's ahead? It really comes down to just one goal, and it seems to influence everything else. My goal this year: to keep living. While trying to be a good person. I am going to try to do all I can, every day, to be better than the day before. I'm going to say my prayers. Thank God for opportunities. Read with my kids. Walk outdoors. Smile. Help someone. Only speak kindness. There—now I've written it down. So maybe I've got a chance at achieving it.

Immunity Idol.

My kids love watching the reality show *Survivor.* Even though I now feel like a survivor, I would not survive one day on that show. They make a living backbiting, eating weird things, sleeping outside, and wearing bikinis—four things I try to avoid. Most of these characters spend a good portion of their days searching for the hidden immunity idol, granting them the supreme power to not be eliminated so no matter how mean they are, they get to stick around.

A strange thing happened to me after Kevin died. I found myself thinking, *This is it—this is the trial I've been given to bear.* I certainly don't remember signing up for it, so I'm assuming it was assigned to me. And my thought continued—*If I endure this trial, and not just endure but face it with patience and cheerfulness, then the Lord will only pour out blessings on me.* That's when inspiration struck—I had found the immunity idol!!! Nothing else could happen to us. My family and I were immune to any more heartbreak or pain. Losing a spouse—our family's dad—was certainly enough of a trial and heartache to bear the rest of our lives, right?!

This proved true for a few months. Our family was nothing but blessed. More than blessed. Every week was like winning the lotto as friends and anonymous donors generously spoiled our family. A year of free housecleaning! An all-expense-paid family trip to a ski resort! Five roundtrip tickets to Washington, D.C.! I realize how far this is from typical, how unbelievably fortunate we were to have happened to plop down in life amid an overtly generous community. I couldn't make sense of it any more than I could that I was a widow. Even while writing on my donated thank you cards, I had a hard time finding the right words to thank people who donated things such as thank you cards, Christmas trees, and funds for my children's future, mostly because my mind and my heart struggled with why there would be such a thing as a Kevin Hegewald Memorial Fund. I felt so unworthy of the attention, like I was somehow reaping rewards Kevin had earned.

Even with all of the help and support of family, friends, and Mr. Anonymous, the way I felt most blessed after Kevin died was that my children continued to do well in school and continue to make good decisions. I try not to take this for granted. I've certainly been shown that there are other options in the world of how to cope with something tragic, and I'm grateful that my children haven't taken those paths. Smiling and being happy comes so innately to each one of them, I wonder if they even consider it a choice.

Shortly after my first holiday season without Kevin, on a flight from Salt Lake City back home to Orange County, my eyes were opened to an alternative way to deal with tragedy from a fellow comrade still searching for her immunity idol. I had escaped for a quick weekend to celebrate my parent's 50th wedding anniversary. It was terrifying flying all by myself as I'm already a little fearful of planes, to put it lightly. I'm actually one step below full-on panic-attack-needs-to-be-escorted-off-the-plane-in-a-wheelchair-wearing-an-oxygen-mask lady. I don't feel anxious the entire time we're in the air—just at take off, touch down, and any time that I can actually feel the airplane moving. My coping technique is to not take my eyes off of the flight attendants. I figure that if they're not panicking, I shouldn't either. I realize they are trained professionals who daily plaster looks of "all is under control" on their faces, along with their foundation. But it's a great indication that it's time to start praying when they head to the back of the plane mid-flight to put on their own seat belts. The worst part of flying with all my children with me is that I have to pretend that I'm not terrified. They all just think I have an odd fascination with the flight crew.

But here I was, flying solo. I had no one who I needed to be brave for. I started praying when I first stepped on the plane, "Please don't crash—my kids will be orphans. Please have the pilot be sober. Please have confident stewardesses. Please serve more than just peanuts." When I found my aisle seat, I looked at my seatmate, and saw that she was crying. We were in for a long flight.

Ah, how I love the beauty of distraction. When my new best friend was fifteen, she left home and got a job at a local mill. She continued to go to high school, won Homecoming Queen, got serious with a boyfriend, and became pregnant. She went to the courts and was granted a legal divorce from her mom and her stepdad so she could make the worst decision of her life and marry the guy who was responsible. Five years later, she had two children, she was still working at the mill, and she was divorced from the bum who refused to get off the couch. On Christmas Eve, she found herself completely alone, alienated from all family, and without her kids as they were with their bum dad.

"What did you do?!" I begged her to continue. My eyes hadn't looked once at the stewardesses.

"I drank myself unconscious."

By the time she woke up, Christmas was over.

Her answer was mind-blowing. Was that an option?! I had never thought of that. I realized, just as I didn't consider drinking myself unconscious as an option, maybe my kids didn't consider not doing well in school or no longer happily living their lives as options either.

But then one day, my illusions of being untouchable all came crashing down. Literally. It was Valentine's Day. My children and I were sitting around a lovingly set table, enjoying a favorite dinner I had spent my afternoon preparing. If Kevin were still alive, the scenario would have been the same. We would not have quarantined ourselves in a quaint little restaurant enjoying a romantic dinner for two, but we'd be at the kitchen table surrounded by the four little people that somehow were created without having to have romantic dinners for two. I had spent the day trying to remind myself of this fact and focusing all of my energy into recreating a happy moment for my children despite the huge empty space at the table. As we were reading valentines listing the small things we love and admire most about one another, I remember thinking how blessed I am to love, and be loved, by these people.

And then it happened. A china plate fell to the hard tile floor. I just sat there and watched in slow motion as pieces of blue and white china shattered and scattered everywhere. I was in shock. Just like that, my immunity—gone. Shattered were the illusions that my life would only be blessed and be void of future pain. I jumped up and with a dustpan, swept up the broken pieces of china and dashed dreams. Of course, the dreams of raising my children with a partner, having financial stability, and growing old with someone died with Kevin on September 20th. But, now, so were the dreams of a life untouched by future heartache. As I dumped the shards in the trash can, the realization crept in and planted itself that maybe there would be more broken plates in my life after that. But maybe I'd only have to endure each tragedy once. Funny thing is, I accidentally broke another plate the very next week. Probably just to make sure I got the message. But all that was before the whole china cabinet came crashing down.

As we emerged from the holidays, I don't know which stunk more—literally: the rat who had taken up residence in the engine of my minivan or the mold that was discovered growing on the back sides of all of my kitchen cabinets after our water pipe had burst … for the second time. When the restoration company called to report that the water damage repair would cost between ten and twenty thousand, I learned my reaction was not typical. The bearer of bad news on the other end of the phone was startled by my calm response and inquired, "Are you okay? You seem to be handling this really well."

After Kevin died, I might not have gained immunity, but at least I had found perspective.

Today, I Laughed.

No Mountain Too High. Tuesday, February 28, 2012.

So now it's time again for the annual girls' trip. My mom flew in to watch my kids so I could escape to ... Disneyland. I suppose my friends thought a new widow and "the happiest place on earth" were a good combination. Knowing my fear of roller coasters, Ben asked me, "What are YOU going to do?" I wasn't worried. I am very happy waiting and watching others torture themselves.

A day at Disneyland without children? There was no whining, crying, complaining, or "how much longer?" There were still probably just as many restroom stops, but no one needed to be reminded to wash their hands. We were indifferent to the length of lines as conversations remained uninterrupted whether standing, waiting, walking, or even riding. The finale of the day was Space Mountain. There was no pressure, prodding, teasing, or begging from my friends to join them. Only acceptance. I wouldn't have expected anything different. These are the same friends who I can say never put me in a situation I didn't want to be in during the tumultuous years of high school. Maybe that's why I decided to join them. Maybe I didn't want to sit through Captain EO again while I was waiting. Maybe I had a momentary lapse of good judgment. Whatever the reason, I climbed aboard. The ride started and the scream that escaped my throat could hardly be described as human. When I stopped screaming just long enough to take a breath, I heard the friend sitting next to me say, "This is actually kind of fun." "Could this actually be fun?" I wondered ... right before the ride catapulted into louder, darker, and faster. The ride is all one big black-and-white blur. I vaguely recall profanity flying from my lips, but either it was absorbed by the deafening noise of the ride or my friends were laughing too hysterically to hear it because they made no mention of it. I survived and emerged triumphant. Later retelling the harrowing details to my children, I became their hero.

I can't think of better friends to ride Space Mountain with. Together we've survived and supported one another through a lot of ups and downs—disappointments, divorce, the loss of a parent, a child, and most recently, a spouse. These are the friends who flew in for Kevin's funeral, then packed up all of the photos and Kevin paraphernalia, and took it all back to display in Salt Lake City for the repeat performance. They embody the very best qualities, but the thing I appreciate and love the very most about them ... they make me laugh. Maya Angelou said, "My great hope is to laugh as much as I cry." Not me. I hope to laugh much, much more than I cry. Stepping off that roller coaster, I knew I had achieved what I thought to be impossible a year ago—I laughed.

Widow Perks.

Just as there are perks to having cancer, there are a few perks to being a widow, though not nearly as glamorous. Namely, I do get a large showing of carolers at Christmas. Living in an area where the average age seems to be eighteen, widows are hard to find. I have even had carloads of carolers drive in from neighboring areas in search of a widow. Let's just say my fake smile gets a lot of practice standing at the door by myself (my kids all seem to disappear at the faintest sound of fa-la-las), listening to a joyous crowd spreading holiday cheer.

In contrast to the cancer card, which allows you to do whatever you want, the widow card allows you to NOT do whatever you want. Baby showers, birthday lunches, multi-level marketing parties, book clubs, school committees; I have a "get out of jail free" card that allows me to not participate in any of it! What's even better is I don't even have to say no because no one even dares to ask. And it's a good thing because if they did, I would have to say no. Either way, everyone is understanding and forgiving. If I do happen to show up to an event outside of my own home, I am treated like a special guest just for gracing them with my appearance. I think they like seeing I'm still alive.

But, there is a catch. Unlike the cancer card, which seems to have no expiration date (unless the person expires themself), the widow card does. I should clarify: the forty-three-year-old widow card does. Slowly, I have been dragged back into the real world with real people where I am expected to carry on real conversations about which color of paint would look best in the guest room and which basketball team would provide the better chance of going pro. I'm trying my best.

Another widow perk related to the "Don't show up to anything" allowance is the "If I do show up, I'm going to be late" mentality. After forty-two years of always being punctual (I was even born right on my due date), that first year, I maintained a perfect record of never showing up on time. Kevin would be so proud. Kevin's inability to be on time was the number one argument in our nineteen years of marriage. Our professions added to the dichotomy: in Kevin's emergency room world, patients wait for the doctor, not the other way around. In my mom profession world, school bells demanding tardy slips and fifteen minute swimming lessons that cost thirty dollars motivate you to not be a single minute late, ever. Sometimes I wonder now that Kevin is gone if it was silly of me to always be upset at him for being late. But I'm more upset at myself that I didn't learn much earlier in our marriage that he wasn't ever going to change, so I should just get over it. I think Kevin somehow knew deep down inside that he had to live life in double time. It's rather ironic that Kevin left too early.

Relying on parenting help from the other side is a pretty awesome perk. Not many people can say to their teenage son as he walks out the door, "Remember, I can't see what you're doing, but your dad can." We all take turns claiming posthumous Kevin. I will announce out loud, "Okay, Ben, it's your turn to take Dad to science camp with you." or "Sophie, it looks like Dad will be with you on your eighteen-mile hike." I feel good about these declarations; Kevin loved to be involved with anything in the great outdoors. And while I'm trying to remind my children that their dad is still there, the announcement is more for the benefit of Kevin, whom I am assuming still needs to be told what is going on and where he needs to be. Some things don't change.

We have had an episode of heavenly intervention. I promised my daughter that I would never talk about this incident, but I also promised her a house where she wouldn't have to share a bathroom with her brothers. Shucks. We had just arrived in Washington, D.C. for spring break, six months after Kevin had passed away. In a lapse of good judgment, I told my fifteen-year-old that she could drive the rental car forward a few feet so we could load our luggage in the trunk. I'm hoping for this next part you happen to be one of the billion people familiar with the *Twilight* series. Remember when Edward, with skin like porcelain, stops the car from crushing Bella with his two bare hands and his lightning speed vampire abilities? Let's just say, Kevin totally did that! That is the only possible explanation as to why our rental car, with Sophie taking an aggressive punch on the gas pedal, stopped just centimeters from crashing into a parked car. Sophie describes this episode by saying, "It's the only time I've been grateful that Dad was on the other side."

With all of the genuine widow perks, let me put to rest some of the perceived ones. Having a king sized bed all to myself? With four kids—hasn't happened yet. Not having to cook dinner every night? With four kids—hasn't happened yet. Sole possession of the remote control? With four kids—hasn't happened yet. And always getting to be right? Not as great as you think it would be; plus, I have four kids, so that hasn't happened yet either.

Milestones.
No Mountain Too High. Tuesday, March 20, 2012.

Milestones: Events that mark a significant change.
Kidney stones: A hard mass formed in the kidneys.
Miles apart in meaning, but both can be painful to pass.

Today marks six months. Odd to think we have been without Kevin the same number of months as he was ill. Not sure which 6 months felt longer; guess it depends if you ask me or Kevin. Since September 20th, we have been hitting some big milestones pretty fast. The first one was three days later to be exact. We celebrated Ben's 10th birthday at the beach the night before Kevin's funeral. Then came Sam's 8th birthday and baptism. Survived Thanksgiving, Christmas, and New Year's, but what I dreaded most was that special holiday in February ... Presidents' Day. We are so passionate about George and Abe that every year we celebrate their births with a ski vacation. Kevin loves this vacation. We escape to the Utah ski slopes where we spend our days skiing and our nights recovering. Kevin is infamous for his ski lift interviews. Anyone who had the pleasure of riding the lift with Kevin also had the pleasure of a video camera in their face. Then, at night we would watch the video and laugh and holler at Kevin for his ridiculous footage which usually showed more sky or snow than skiers.

Fortunately, we have friends who really liked Kevin, and kind of like the rest of us, who invited us for a Presidents' Day ski weekend. Three days of skiing, snowmobiling, sledding, ping-ponging, eating, playing, and very little sleeping—my kids loved it. Kevin would have loved it. I imagined Kevin with the video camera. And even though there was still a lot of snow and sky, I know his eyes were on us—watching me drive his big manly truck in the snow and his four kids carving and falling down the ski slopes, and I know we made him happy because we were doing something he loved.

Looking ahead to the next six months, we have some big milestones. And though feeling a little apprehensive, I need to remember that, just like kidney stones, "This too shall pass."

The Psychic.

I thought the timing was perfect. We were returning home from spring break. Washington, D.C. was incredible, and we had a few hours to kill in the airport during a long layover, so I announced to my children that I had scheduled a family appointment to meet Dave, a very nice psychologist. Indescribable uproar. All at once, each of them expressed their very strong opinions with varying degrees of tears and complaints. A plaintive "I'm NOT going to see some psychic!" turned the conversation into me trying to explain the difference between a psychologist and a psychic, while a side conversation was being carried out over the last television episode of *Psych*, amidst another child doing their best to convince me that they would not be joining the family psychic experience.

At the moment, I actually thought visiting a psychic might be a good idea. Especially if they could tell me if my children were going to turn out all right or if I needed to force them to meet with a psychologist. But trying to convince four very different personalities that creating a relationship with Dave might be beneficial for sometime in the future was not easy. I told my children they had my permission to visit with Dave and talk for the entire hour about how I drive them crazy. One of them pointed out that it would be a little awkward to discuss with Dave that the way I was driving them the most crazy was by making them meet with him.

I had met with Dave before on my own shortly after Kevin passed away. I had visited several psychologists looking for the right fit for someone on whom I could inflict my children. I instantly liked Dave. He is a big, manly-looking man, who has no problem whatsoever letting the tears flow freely. I was most impressed with his ability to continue to speak while he was crying and keep his voice from going to an octave where it is no longer intelligible, which happens to be a very great skill if you're going to be a psychologist. As much as I was there to "interview" Dave, I was really the one being interrogated on how I was handling things. Dave asked about my faith, the traditions we were continuing, the open family discussions we were having. I seemed to have all of the right answers because I heard him announce at the end of our session, "You seem to be doing everything you can to navigate through this." (Yay!) But uh-oh, he continued: "My one suggestion …" (Oh no.) "… is maybe you're a little bit TOO happy." (What?!) "Your kids need to see you cry and hear you say how hard this is. If they only see you being positive all of the time, they are going to wonder what the problem is with them because they're feeling so unhappy." (Ugh.)

Dave's advice was going to be a problem for me. It's not that I can't cry … I just can't cry in front of my children. Or anyone else. Trust me, there have been times in my life when a few tears would have been beneficial. But as a wife and mom, I tended to take a different approach to sharing emotion by stringing together four or five adverbs: "I honestly, really, seriously, sincerely need you to get home on time." And here I was, being advised to abandon my Pollyanna approach.

It's all I knew: take away being happy or, at the very least, pretending to be happy, and I wouldn't survive. My greatest fear was that if I allowed myself to start crying in front of my kids, I wouldn't be able to stop. Ever. That was the beauty of my crying chair. Every morning I was able to get it all out—tears, mucus, digestive secretions—and then move on with my day fluid-free. But, I will do anything for the sake of my kids. If crying every once in a while in front of them was going to help, I was willing to take the risk. I only had Dave to blame a few months later when Sam approached me and took my face in his hands and asked, "Haven't you cried enough?!"

I did drag my kids in for our family psych experience. It was pretty much a disaster. My children didn't particularly enjoy being asked questions like, "So, what do you do when you're feeling sad?" or "What do you think your dad is doing right now?" (By the way, this last question didn't help alleviate Dave of his psychic reputation.) Each of my kids reacted in a way I could have predicted. Josh cried. Sophie was furious as she attempted to answer the questions while holding back tears. Ben was somber and silent. And Sam didn't seem to mind, but only because I had promised that after, we could eat at Ruby's Diner … which ironically ended up being where the most therapeutic discussion took place. What my kids *really* wanted to talk about came right out with our round of Oreo shakes: "Mom, are we going to be poor?"

In the six months since Kevin had died, I had attempted to maintain our same lifestyle to provide a sense of calm and security for my children. Instead, it freaked them out. They were smart enough to recognize that the parent who earned the money was no longer around. And they hadn't seen any signs of job applications, For Sale signs, or that an end to sports, music lessons, or family vacations was coming. As far as they could tell, we were on a fast path to the poor house. In all, they were more interested in discussing not what their dad was doing, but if their mom knew what she was doing.

So over burgers and fries, I taught my children about life insurance, social security death benefits, mortgages, student savings accounts, and my full-time job managing it all. (Of course, I didn't mention the "gap years"—those future years, according to my financial advisor, when I am all out of money and before I can start withdrawing from our retirement fund. Why scare them with that?) I now smirk thinking about our hour session with Dave. Sure, he taught my children how to cope when they feel sad about the past; but there I was providing them the comfort they needed right then—by removing their fear of our future. In an effort to demonstrate to my kids that I take money management seriously, I called and canceled our follow-up appointment with Dave, deciding that money might be better spent on burgers and fries.

Journal.
Wednesday, March 7, 2012.

I would like to announce to the world that my situation is actually getting harder rather than easier. The phrase "time heals all wounds"... so misleading. Time just makes the mind forget. Wounds aren't healed. You just forget the messy details of why you are so wounded. I used to not be able to close my eyes without some pretty graphic images appearing of Kevin in his final hours. Now, I look at the pictures of Kevin in his last weeks and I can't imagine that the human body can even look that way. I am still surrounded by all of his stuff. I look at all of it and I wonder when he's going to come home to use it.

Tasks.

I once heard the advice to never do anything your first week of marriage that you don't want to be stuck doing the rest of your married life. Unfortunately, it was way after my own bridal shower that I heard it. I could have used that one. As a newlywed married to a pre-med student, the household tasks were far from equally divided. I found myself in sole control of keeping dishes clean, toilets scrubbed, and bills paid. As our family grew, so did my list. I became the sole laundress, housemaid, chef, and chauffeur. Kevin maintained control of the yard, which over the years went from the size of a postage stamp, to a small plot of land, to finally a yard that could accommodate two soccer goals, which is when Kevin promptly gave our lawn mower away to the neighborhood gardener, claiming there was no room to store it in the garage. I attempted to use the same excuse with storing the vacuum cleaner, but it didn't work. We store it in the garage.

Over time, Kevin's list grew shorter and shorter. But there were still a few areas I was holding out on, refusing to ever do them even once. One was catching mice.

While living in Loma Linda, we had a few uninvited rodents. The plan was to put out glue traps for mice at night. Kevin would check them early in the morning on his way to the hospital and then again in the evening when he got home. Imagine my dismay when I returned home in the middle of the day with little Joshie and Sophie to find a mouse stuck on the glue trap in the very center of the room on that blasted orange shag carpet. Only its front legs were stuck so it had maneuvered itself across the room and was furiously gnawing off one of its legs to get free. I had a choice: I could either introduce Josh and Sophie to their new three-legged pet, or grab a broom and dustpan to sweep the mouse and glue trap into the trash. Josh and Sophie named him Stumpie … on his way into the can. It was over. I was done for. Kevin the animal lover now knew that given dire circumstances, I would throw out mice. You might think I'm grateful for that experience now that I am the sole mouse catcher of the family. Um no, not really.

Another task I never touched was tickle tackles. This was Kevin's name for wrestling with the kids, or what I considered torturing them. Somehow, tickle tackles made the top ten list of things my kids missed now with Kevin gone. My little kids could hardly wait for their dad to walk in the door and get ready for tickle tackles. All Legos and toys suddenly disappeared to create a large open area in the family room. Kevin would stretch himself out in the middle of the floor and pretend to be taking a nap. As soon as the first brave child crept close enough, Kevin would spring to action and the WWF would occur for the next fifteen minutes, or until someone got hurt, which was usually less time than that. I couldn't stand the screams and shrieks and would usually need to leave the room. If Kevin tried to catch my leg as I was making my escape I would emphatically declare that "Moms DO NOT wrestle!" As much as I hated the noise and the tears, I tolerated it. That's what made their dad coming home from work my kids' favorite part of the day, which perfectly aligned with the advice my grandmother gave me when I was expecting my first child. She said, "The best thing you can do is help your kids love their dad."

She quickly added, "That's the only way you will ever have a quiet moment by yourself."

Shortly after Kevin passed away, I asked the kids what they missed the most. Sam promptly said tickle tackles. I actually debated whether I should get down and tickle tackle with Sam and Ben just so my kids wouldn't grow up to be wimps. But I decided I would rather them be wimps than boys who think they can wrestle girls. So, I'm still staying clear of that one. And even though I now do everything else for them, their dad is the best because he tickle tackled.

Why Not Me.

I never really questioned why the Lord took Kevin instead of me. Although my children probably question it daily. They recognize that the Lord left the dependable and took the fun. They'll probably spend the rest of their lives debating if one is better than the other.

But there are two incidents that cause me to stop and wonder if the man upstairs got it right. Ironically, both occurred on the 24th of July. For forty-nine states, July 24th is just July 24th, but in Utah, July 24th is a reason to make homemade ice cream and light fireworks in celebration of the Mormon pioneers entering the Utah valley.

As I was born two days after July 4th, I've always delighted in our family tradition of lighting fireworks on my birthday. Once I was married, Kevin eagerly took the responsibility from my three younger brothers of providing the fireworks show. No one in the Cannon family will ever forget the firework production of 2005 that Kevin performed at the beach house in the Outer Banks. It wasn't the fireworks that were captivating; Kevin was the real show. He had spent the afternoon building bunkers with my brothers out of boogie boards and sand. We watched with pure fascination as Kevin, sporting a headlamp, would ignite a series of fireworks and then run for cover and dive behind the bunker while screaming, "FIRE IN THE HOLE!"

A no less entertaining performance occurred the year Kevin drove me to North Beach in San Clemente and ignited (one by one) thirty-five illegal Roman candles—one for each year of my life. While observing all of this with my children from the front seat of our car, which was idling for a quick escape, I wondered how my innocent childhood tradition had become all knotted up with doing something that could land us in jail. Kevin would only declare it was worth it.

Which is why, when our family was in Salt Lake City, Utah on July 24th, before leaving for our last Outer Banks vacation, Kevin chose to leave the bed he had been resting on all evening. A little bit of rain, and a little more wind, did not deter my Aunt Kathleen from proceeding with the promised fireworks show, and a little cancer sickness would not deter Kevin from watching. We observed with interest as Aunt Kath walked out to the middle of her cul-de-sac and set up two ladders with a board running across the tops of the two. With such a large crowd of relatives, she wanted the display to be centered and spectacular for everyone to see. A bucket was placed on top of the board, filled with bottle rockets, and the fuses were lit. In a detrimental split second, this party changed from just a typical family gathering to one that will go down in the Cannon archives. The bucket tipped, and we watched with horror and some guilty excitement as the first bottle rocket blasted towards the neighbor's open garage door, exploding underneath his parked car. The awesome sight and the explosive sound had diverted our attention from the tipped bucket of lit bottle rockets. With each jolt, the bucket rotated, firing the next bottle rocket into new territory. Only after watching the next bottle rocket explode in the same neighbor's front bush, did we realize that the next lit rocket was aimed directly at the gawking spectators. I am not proud of my actions—I bolted. Apparently, according to Kevin, I even knocked into my sick husband, who was leaping towards the innocent children (mine included) sitting on the curb watching the lethal show. Kevin had the opposite instinct I had—while I clamored to save myself, Kevin's reflex was to save the kids. I'd love to give full credit to Kevin's emergency medicine instincts, but it was most likely that Kevin is just a really good person. It is this moment that made me wonder if God had made a mistake and was in fact taking the wrong person. It wasn't until the fireworks were extinguished, and a few quick brushes with fire assessed, that I stopped to analyze the situation. Racked with shame of how truly deserving I was of the bad mom award, I asked my kids what they did when the flames came flying. I was blessed to hear they all took off running, too! Right behind me!! So maybe I'm not such a bad mom after all. I may be self-preserving, but at least I have taught my kids to follow.

I'd like to state my defense upfront for this next incident. First of all, this never would have happened if Kevin were still alive. Secondly, my intentions were innocent—I was only aiming to create a memorable activity. And third, no one died.

In the spirit of trying to celebrate Utah Pioneer Day 2012 in California, I thought it would be fun for the kids to make homemade taffy—a pioneer staple. The ingredients were simple: sugar, water, corn syrup, salt, glycerin*, vanilla, and butter. I was mindful of the asterisk and read, "*Glycerin can be purchased from a drugstore and is an important ingredient in this recipe." Lucky me, being married to a doctor/cancer patient, we still had a virtual drugstore in our own home. Sure enough, I found a bottle of glycerin in our medicine cabinet. The taffy was a disaster: too runny to even handle, so not a bite was enjoyed. It wasn't until the following day when Sophie offered to attempt the taffy project again that she showed me the label on the glycerin bottle. Big, bold letters spelled the words, "FOR EXTERNAL USE ONLY," with a warning on the back label to call the poison control center if accidentally ingested. I turned where everyone else turns when they don't have a doctor in the house—the internet. I googled, "Can you eat glycerin?" Up popped my answer: "It's the glycerin you find on the cake-making aisle at the grocery store, you idiot!" (It seriously said that. I wonder how many rude teenagers they hire to answer questions at Google.) The next day, after purchasing the correct glycerin from the local craft store, the taffy still turned out runny. I cut my losses. I figured I should just buy a bag of taffy from the grocery store and be grateful that I hadn't accidentally poisoned my children. As I was the only one left in charge.

Sam Says the Darnedest Things.

Wednesday, March 14, 2012.

Today Sam asked me a hard question. I was working outside with my head down and my hands in the garden when Sam said, "Mom, do you think you will get another husband?" My first thought: I'm so glad he can't see the shocked expression on my face. My second thought: approach this seriously.

"Sam," I said, looking him straight in the eyes, "Right now, I really don't think so. Is that okay with you?"

"Well ..." Sam said, "I just sometimes think our family feels small. But, I don't know how it happens—do you find someone who is just him without a family?"

What I wanted to say was "Yes, that's exactly what you do." What I actually said was "When a lot of people get married again, they marry someone who also has a family and then they have one really big family combined."

"Oh. Well, do you think we should adopt a baby and a husband? I have always wanted a baby girl and I would play with her all of the time, and sometimes I feel so lonely ... "

This is where I had to cut in, "Lonely?! But there are still five of us. And are you trying to adopt a husband, too?"

"Well, I don't know how that part really works. But I would really, really like a baby sister."

June Gloom.

San Clemente has earned its title as bearer of "the most temperate climate in the U.S.," with highs that range from 68-80 and lows that range from 44-61. Here, you can expect to enjoy sunny, blue skies year round…except in June. The locals accurately describe the fog that rolls in each morning from the ocean to never burn off throughout the day as "June Gloom." There could not exist a more accurate description of the way I feel about June. Just like the anticipated weather, after Kevin died, June Gloom rolled in on June 1st with the annual Fathers and Sons campout and never burned off the entire month, leaving me enveloped in a grief-filled fog.

A suggestion from Dave the psychic was that I create some family traditions where we could remember Kevin—to love him and celebrate his life, but also to grieve his absence. June provided ample opportunities to do that. In fact, we could devote the entire third week of June to remembering Kevin. The week's line up began on Sunday celebrating Father's Day, followed by Kevin's birthday on the 19th, the nine-month mark of his passing on the 20th, and finishing off strong on Saturday, June 23rd, with our twentieth wedding anniversary.

Now, I've survived hell week before. But the last hell week I remember included being dropped off at a local mall wearing my pajamas with all of my new sorority sisters and no ride home until we had solicited $5.00 from strangers in exchange for kisses. My new hell week did not include any random acts of lasciviousness, but it seemed like the perfect opportunity to schedule a family breakdown.

I have personally scheduled a breakdown before. Christmas, 2006. I had just arrived home from a holiday party when I announced to Kevin, "I want to go see a psychiatrist."

"Why?"

"I think I'm going to have a nervous breakdown." I said it casually, as if it were a lunch date I was scheduling on the calendar. Only my calendar had been inundated those past few years with appointments with endocrinologists, oncologists, obstetricians, and realtors.

"Why don't you go visit a psychologist or a counselor instead?"

"Because I need drugs."

It's true. I needed to see a psychiatrist because I needed to be handed a happy little prescription for my imminent nervous breakdown.

I can't remember the opening question Dr. G asked me. But I do remember pretty much talking the rest of the hour about my life the past few years. I warmed up with the details of my five-year- old daughter being diagnosed with type 1 diabetes, honing the new skills I was required to master of giving insulin shots and testing blood sugar, and the rigid eating schedule I now needed to adhere to—an eating schedule that became even more complicated when she required a gluten-free diet after being diagnosed with celiac disease. I advanced to the details of my husband being diagnosed six months later with a rare cancer in his leg and the year of my life that was physically exhausting due to chemotherapy, radiation, and doctor appointments, and emotionally exhausting from the fear of losing Kevin—both exhaustions exasperated by the fact that I was pregnant with our fourth child. I threw in the details of the stress we felt from a personal lawsuit against Kevin for a wrongful death in the emergency room and the financial stress we suffered from carrying two mortgages for nine months after moving into our dream home without first selling our original dream home.

When I finally came up for air, I half expected Dr. G to pick up the phone and call Oprah to inform her that he had found her next guest. Instead, he said, "And how is your life now?"

"My life is great."

That was my problem. My life was then great. Sophie was healthy and managing diabetes and celiac disease beautifully. Kevin was alive, had hit his two year mark of being cancer free, and still had both of his legs attached to his body. The lawsuit was settled outside of court and Kevin was found at no fault. And our sweet little Samuel completed our happy family, in a new home and neighborhood we had grown to love. So that was the big question: "If my life is so great, then why am I about to have a nervous breakdown?!?"

Dr. G's answer was simple: "Because now you can."

At the end of our session, I got my drugs—mission accomplished. It took me about six months to feel stable again. It was quite a procedure to unload the burdens I had been carrying and the emotions I had been suppressing and to slowly come to accept the fact that now my life was great. Of course, six weeks alone on a beach in Southern France would have had the same result in a much shorter amount of time, but Dr. G had only handed me a prescription, not an airline ticket.

Scheduling a personal breakdown is one thing; it is far more difficult to schedule an entire family breakdown. I had to look ahead at all of the busy schedules and make sure there weren't any important activities that would be missed or altogether forgotten because we were unavailable from our dark black hole. Unfortunately, when I looked at the calendar, I realized the third week of June coincided with Josh and Sophie's high school finals week. Well, I guess that proved it—it would be the perfect hell week after all.

I understand that all breakdowns can't be scheduled. The spontaneous ones happen all the time. An unexpected photo of Kevin posted by a friend on Facebook or a beloved song of Kevin's played on the radio would instantly send my teenagers off the edge into a pit of despair. As much as it broke my heart, I was actually relieved to find them sobbing in their bedrooms. It provided me with the comforting reassurance that they were going to be okay; they were going to get through this. I believe that if they never fell into the black hole, their grief and sadness and anger would only grow deeper and they wouldn't ever know the feeling of their Savior rescuing them from it.

But I couldn't depend on a random incident to spark our family breakdown. I needed to take control … without my children knowing that my intention was to create a potential meltdown. One night around the dinner table, I was handed the golden opportunity I had been searching for to discuss the upcoming hell week's activities.

TableTopic: "If you could create a holiday, what would it be and what would you do?"

"Let's have a Kevin Hegewald holiday!" I proposed.

I rushed ahead, "We can eat his favorite foods!" But when tuna steaks, sauerkraut, and tomato salad were all thrown out as Kevin's favorite foods, we quickly threw out the idea of us having to eat them.

"How about his favorite dessert?" That one was easier to accommodate with his second favorite dessert, cheesecake, overriding his top choice of peach cobbler.

I forged ahead, "What do you think we should do?"

Mumbled suggestions included going on a hike, or visiting Kevin's Crag—his favorite surf spot that he named after himself.

"What if we watch some home videos?" That did it. Any support I had rallied for my first annual Kevin Hegewald Day disappeared.

Josh took the lead as spokesman: "NO! If you do that, I'm not coming."

I heard three others echo, "Me neither!"

Then inspiration hit me: ping pong. Kevin loved to play ping pong. He was raised with a ping pong paddle in his hand and tried his best to bring honor to his ping pong heritage. (His eighty-year-old German father beat an eighteen-year-old Russian to claim the title of "Ping Pong Champion" on a Carnival Cruise. We affectionately call the event World War III.) Acquiring an outdoor ping pong table would be the perfect way to honor Kevin.

The big unveiling on Father's Day was exciting for about five minutes until we opened the box and watched hundreds of bolts and screws spew out onto the ground. Visions of a delightful afternoon of playing ping pong together as a family vanished. And any smidgeon of hope of attempting to put it together ourselves was dashed when it was discovered that the instructions were in German. (Nice one, Kevin.) My kids yelled out, "Where's Dad when we need him?!"

Thanks to a good friend, who is as competent at putting together ping pong tables as he is at treating injured people in the emergency room, the table was assembled and ready for action two days later on Kevin's birthday. We held the first annual Kevin Hegewald Ping Pong Tournament, also known as "KHPPT." The brackets were fierce with single elimination. Josh came out on top, barely sweeping by Ben, who proved he has a strong chance of usurping the championship bragging rights the year following. That ping pong table turned out to be a miracle. I'm not just referring to the fact that our non-German speaking friend was able to put it together. That table united our family, doing something our dad had loved. Eating cheesecake while laughing and being silly and playing ping pong with my children … I know it was Kevin's birthday we were celebrating, but I was the one who received a gift. A much-needed moment of joy.

Still Standing.

We survived that ominous third week of June together as a family despite being blindsided by some unexpected heartaches. I dragged my kids to a different church service just so I wouldn't have to watch my own kids take the stand and sing the traditional Father's Day songs with all of the youth at our church. I thought I'd be okay to watch other kids do it, just not mine. I was wrong. Turns out, it was still hard. I also wasn't prepared for the homemade, heartfelt Father's Day crafts constructed at school for their dad that were handed to me instead. Ironically, the hardest day during that third week of June didn't turn out to be Father's Day, or Kevin's birthday, or the nine month mark of his passing, or our 20th wedding anniversary, but my kids' last day of school.

During a university study abroad, I remember standing at the foot of the great pyramid of Giza in Egypt and marveling at something so tremendous in size and ancient in date. The sheer magnitude of the size was impossible to conceive without actually standing next to it and inhaling dust that seemed to have been present since the beginning of time. Having enough manpower to build the pyramids seems inconceivable, and though contradicting theories exist on how they were actually constructed, they all agree that they were built one stone at a time.

It's a humbling moment to step back and realize you have made it through an entire school year by taking it just one day at a time. On their last day of school, I looked at my kids with present eyes and realized that while I was surviving this past year day by day, they had done exactly what I am always telling them NOT to do: they had grown up. I was more in awe at that moment than when standing at the foot of the great pyramid. I realized that, just like the pyramids, my kids are still standing. They could have collapsed into a pile of rubble, but instead they were living, breathing, smiling, good-report-card-wielding human beings. I was the one who crumbled into the arms of both Ben and Sam's school teachers—teachers who had endured this past year with us and had made school a safe place for my kids to grow up when I had needed that time to fall down every day at my crying chair.

Sam Says the Darnedest Things.
Thursday, August 2, 2012.

Sam: I had the BEST dream! Dad was still alive. I tried to stay asleep and not wake up.
Mom: Was he healthy or sick?
Sam: He was in a wheelchair.
Mom: Oh, so he was sick, but he was still alive, huh?
Sam: Yeah. He gave me a movie to watch—and it was a real one! That one where people said, "The thing I remember most about Kevin Hegewald." But Dad gave it to me and told me that now I could remember him.

Garage.

I love to be organized the same way I love to breathe. Both come second nature to me, and both seem to be my prescription for survival. The clothes in my closet are organized by color, the books on my bookshelves are alphabetized, and on a good day, my Tupperware is all stacked and sorted by size. I live in a home where everything has its place, and if it doesn't have a place … it's put in the garage.

There are so many positive advantages of living in Southern California that I try not to complain about the not-so-great things, such as the cost of living, the education system, and the governor. Actually, I do complain about those things. But I choose not to broadcast the disadvantage of not having a basement in my house for storage. That's apparently what garages are for in California. Our garage is filled with the ordinary bikes, skateboards, surfboards, garden tools, and camping equipment of every all-American garage, but ours also houses holiday decorations, food storage, thirty wicker baskets from our wedding (don't ask), an electronic keyboard, three bar stools that might be the right height in our next home, and everything else that Kevin refused to throw away. As you can guess, there is no room for cars in the garage. That's okay; even with an empty garage, they're both too long to fit anyway. So they're both parked in the driveway, which brings me full circle to one of the greatest advantages of living in a place where the weather is kind to your cars parked outside year-round.

After Kevin passed away, nothing gave me greater anxiety than pulling into my driveway and watching the garage door slowly go up, exposing a garage packed with stuff. And not just stuff—Kevin's stuff. I would quickly dash inside my tidy home, hoping to ignore all of the mess that was making a mess of my heart.

Ten months. That's how long it took me after Kevin died to face the task of cleaning out the garage. I was definitely venturing into unfamiliar territory. But it was time to familiarize myself with all of this manly garage stuff that was bulging out of cupboards and ceiling racks.

My plan of attack was to start with just one little unintimidating cabinet in the corner of the garage. Upon opening the small cabinet door, I was greeted with a smell of dirt and fertilizer and a large plastic Breyers vanilla ice cream container. Unlike the clear plastic tubs I use for organizing, Kevin used any container salvaged from the recycling garbage can, which added to the mystery of what was stored inside. Prying off the lid, I exposed a hundred little packages of opened seeds containing every imaginable variety of vegetables and flowers—a little piece of Kevin's soul.

Kevin loved working in the garden. The days he wasn't at the hospital, that was most likely where you would find him. This was keenly observed by Sam when he was three-years-old. One Sunday, Sam's teacher at church was sharing with the class that Sam's dad was a doctor. Sam corrected her, "My dad's not a doctor—he's a gardener." Kevin's love of gardening was inherited from his father. One year, Kevin attempted to have us renew his childhood tradition of kneeling down in the garden as a family and praying that it might be a bounteous harvest. However, unlike his father's expansive garden that was depended upon to provide a year's worth of food, Kevin's 3x3 garden plot was more to be admired than eaten.

I cried when I opened that bucket of seeds, which confirmed that the seeds would no longer sprout because, right then and there, I certainly over-watered them. It took a moment, but I eventually convinced myself that I didn't need to keep the opened packages of outdated seeds. I had unearthed something much better—years of memories of my favorite gardener. I found the strength to put the seeds in the trash and move on to the next mysterious container.

It took me all week to sort through the garage, and I cried many more buckets of tears. I cried myself distraught when I opened a large container of camping gear—a propane grill, a frying pan and spatula, matches, rain ponchos, a machete, and a plastic tablecloth with fancy clips to keep it from flying off a picnic table. Obviously Kevin camped in style and somehow thought a machete might come in handy. I cried for my kids, mourning the end of their camping adventures with their dad. I left everything packaged in the box and relabeled it: Emergency Supplies. (An emergency being the only time *I* would ever use those things.)

I cried over soccer cleats. You've heard the expression, "It takes a village." Kevin was willing and able to outfit our entire village with sports equipment. I always found it ironic when I would see a neighborhood child decked in pads from head to toe by Kevin, while our own kids remained exposed. Though we had plenty to spare. In my excavation, after each of my children chose one bike helmet, one pair of cleats, and one set of pads, I ended up donating seven bike helmets, eight pairs of soccer cleats, four baseball mitts, four wetsuits, two pairs of swim fins, nine soccer balls, and five sets of skateboarding pads … to a small Mexican village.

Probably the greatest hidden treasure was found inside one of Kevin's travel bags. I discovered a colored picture of our family from five-year-old Sophie, with scrawled letters, "Welcome Home Dad." I'm not sure if I cried more because of how endearing that was for him to keep it all of those years or that we would never again be welcoming him home.

Although I have one box of unidentifiable items that remains for me to sift through someday when I feel ready, I have familiarized myself with all of the manly stuff that's possessing my garage. Now when the garage door goes up, I no longer panic—I feel like Kevin is welcoming me home.

Lessons Learned.

It was coming—the day I'd been dreading and yet dreaming about—the one year mark. I had never been more anxious nor relieved to have a day come. Kind of like giving birth to a baby. We'd been checking off the twentieth of each month for the past eleven months, and we had survived—every season, every holiday, every birthday, every big event, and every insignificant event … without Kevin.

The only other person who was as cognizant of the date as us was my sister-in-law, Jenni. Over the past year, she had been marking the milestones of her family's latest addition, Amelia, born September 20, 2011. Our family loved the visual of Uncle Kevin and baby Amelia slapping five on his departure from—and her arrival to—the world. While I had been chalking off each month as one more month survived, Jenni had been recording the monthly milestones of sitting, crawling, eating, walking, and talking. I think we would both agree that in some ways the year felt like a blink. Jenni blinked and probably wondered when her little baby disappeared and when this moving, babbling human being appeared. I blinked and wondered how one year could have passed when I still felt as hollow and heartbroken as though it happened yesterday. Although, there were signs that healing was taking place. Someone removed the cinder blocks that were attached to my legs, and I started running again. Much like Amelia, I might have been babbling, but I was moving. Of course, by then I'd been told by someone with experience that the second year is actually harder than the first. As incomprehensible as that sounded at the time, I've since found that to be true. Kevin's repeat performance with cancer proved that anyone can survive something difficult once; it's having to go through it again that's hardest.

One of the themes of my Survive the First Year could be "What was I thinking?" Top of the list, obviously, is two funerals. Please, no one ever attempt to do that. Seriously, just don't. There were other blips.

Purchasing tickets for the five of us to see *Wicked* during Christmas break seemed like a brilliant idea to create a memorable and uplifting experience. However, the day was not without its glitches. First, we arrived a few minutes late (thanks to the new me). Once we were escorted into the dark theater and took our seats, I wondered why I had intentionally put myself in a position where I'd feel the sharp pain of Kevin's absence. He loved music and musicals. And the music in *Wicked* already brought me to tears. In such a fragile state, there was a risk that if I started to cry, I'd eventually be escorted out of the theater for making too much noise. So I held my breath. Longest two-and-a-half hours of my life.

After the show, we drove to the Los Angeles LDS temple to see the Christmas lights—something we had enjoyed doing as a family with Kevin the previous year. We had a wonderful time taking pictures and even reenacting a few scenes from the year before, but, unfortunately, Sam accidentally tripped a fuse scuffling with Ben, and half the lights in a section of trees went dark. This led to me fussing at Sam, which led to him asking a homeless grandma who was walking by if she would like to be his new mom. I ended the day crying in my closet. This time, Josh caught me. When he asked me what was wrong, all I could say was "It was such an awesome day—your dad would have loved it."

The most recent "What was I thinking?" moment happened on a Monday night during our weekly family night. Earlier that morning when I got back from a much-needed run, I sat down and wrote a list of truths I had discovered during the last year. I thought with the one year mark just a few days away, this would be a great way for my family to reflect back on the past year and hopefully see some of the positive lessons we'd learned. How this exercise played in my head and how it went down were two different things. That evening, I pulled out the big white board ready to write down the list of all the things my kids would share, and instead, all I heard were four heartbroken children sobbing because their dad was gone. I added one more item to my lessons learned list: it might take a lifetime for my children to see any positive effects of such a devastating experience. For a seventeen, fifteen, ten, and eight-year-old, all that had been learned came at much too great a cost. I threw out my agenda and joined my children in their sorrow.

Lessons Learned

1. Life is short.
2. Life is sometimes unfair.
3. Death can be peaceful.
4. The spirit lives after the mortal body dies.
5. Angels are real.
6. Jesus Christ has felt my pain.
7. Prayers are answered, but not immediately, and not always the way we want.
8. If you pray for comfort, you will always receive it.
9. Healing takes a long time.
10. Miracles happen.
11. People are generous.
12. Sometimes the most unexpected generosity comes from the most unexpected people.
13. No act of service is too small.
14. Ordinary things can prepare you for extraordinary experiences.
15. Crying makes you feel better.
16. Sometimes crying doesn't help.
17. Everyone shows grief differently.
18. Grief is much deeper than sadness.
19. God is mindful of our needs.
20. You can survive a whole year taking it one day at a time.
21. Fear will dissipate when scriptures are opened.
22. No one really knows what to do or say, so don't expect them to.
23. Journals are invaluable.
24. Be grateful for every day.

One Year.

September 20, 2012 began with a rainbow and ended with a sunset. My children and I woke up to a large colorful rainbow taped to our garage door. Supposedly, the day Kevin died there was a beautiful rainbow in the sky over our home that our neighbor captured with her camera. I didn't see it; I was a little preoccupied inside. But this paper rainbow was covered with love messages from friends and neighbors who not only remembered the rainbow, they remembered Kevin.

I wanted to do something adventurous to commemorate the one year anniversary—something thrilling. Something that would be a tribute to Kevin's zeal for life. So I called my kids out of school for the day (citing the reason as a mental health day) and arranged a balloon ride. Now before you start to think how awesome I am, I need to clarify that the balloon was helium and remained tethered to the ground. It was the perfect amount of Kevin and Abby: Kevin—400 feet in the air, Abby—still attached to the ground.

That evening, the celebration continued with a few families gathering at Kevin's Crag—his favorite beach spot. To get to this little piece of paradise, one must walk a mile on a paved switchback road, and then descend 14,000 stairs. At least, it feels like that many. Especially if you're carrying a folding table or five large foil pans of Kevin's favorite hot Mexican take-out. But once you arrive at the sand, you get it all to yourself. The kids surfed and played in the water, hiked over to the hidden cave, and wrote messages to Kevin with a stick in the sand. But the culminating event was going to be lighting two dozen paper lanterns. I had envisioned watching the lanterns drift up to heaven while floating out to sea. Unfortunately, a few smart people in our group pictured them blowing in the opposite direction towards the multi-million dollar homes on the cliffs behind us, and they talked me out of it. Geez, I missed Kevin. Of course, if Kevin were here he would have given no thought to which way the wind was blowing, and

I would have been the one to kibosh the whole thing. I told you this cancer experience has changed me.

So instead of lighting paper lanterns, we sat on the beach and inhaled the most breath-taking sunset. Even I had to admit that this was a much better way to end the day than with the fire department showing up. The sunset was beautiful. If Kevin was on the sunset committee in heaven, he had perfected his assignment.

When I kissed each of my children that night, I thought about how blessed I am. I am so grateful for the four little people who gave me a reason to get out of bed every day for those first 365 days. And I was grateful to have survived September 20th together.

Miracles.

"There are only two ways to live your life. One is as though nothing is a miracle. The other is as though everything is a miracle."
Albert Einstein

I'm no Einstein, but I can recognize a miracle when I see one, and my life has been blessed with ordinary, and extraordinary, events that are, in fact, miracles. It's a miracle when all of the socks that go into the washing machine come out with a matching pair from the dryer. It's a miracle that my vegetable-hating children still continue to grow. It's a miracle that my computer still works. Same with Josh's truck (or my kids in general). It's a miracle that in our backyard in the hardest patch of dirt known to man, weeds can survive, when nothing else can. It's a miracle when all four of my children, with different ages and interests, all agree on the same television show to watch. It's a miracle each time I go in for a mammogram as I watch the technician try to take nothing and make it into something, only then to flatten it back into nothing. Some days it's a miracle I don't totally lose my mind, and I thank God each day for that because I know that could change tomorrow. And it's a miracle, after surviving years of living with Kevin and wanting to strangle him, that now I don't know how I am going to survive in a world without him.

Kevin has been the center of some pretty extraordinary miracles. During his Cancer Round Two battle, it seemed that just as one tumor would be defeated, the next one would raise its ugly head. A tumor on his clivus, a bone at the base of the skull, had caused him to suffer from double vision. As much as I enjoyed having him tell me that *both* of me looked beautiful, his emergency room patients were not as amused when told they had grown an extra nose. Our short-term solution to dealing with the double vision was for Kevin to sport a cool pair of RayBan sunglasses with one of the inside lenses taped. (I believe it was wearing these glasses that catapulted Kevin to cancer-fighting rock star status.)

Within an hour of completing his final radiation treatment on this vision-busting tumor, a debilitating pain from a tumor in his left shoulder blade surfaced. Kevin panicked as he needed to leave for work immediately. He was no longer able to raise his arm. He had been performing his job with one eye, but he didn't trust himself to be able to perform it with one arm. He said a desperate prayer, asking God for help. The moment the prayer ended, so did Kevin's pain. Well, that is for the eight hour shift he worked. When Kevin returned home that night, the pain resurfaced. But just enough to remind him to call his radiologist in the morning and that miracles do happen.

When Kevin's parents arrived a couple of weeks before Kevin passed away, they brought with them a refreshing optimism that everything would work out. However, they could see from Kevin's physical appearance that his life was truly in the Lord's hands. And because we believe that the Lord's hands can accomplish anything, they continued to pray each day that Kevin would be completely healed, that his healthy body would be restored. This rocked us a little bit. Not because we didn't believe that the Lord was capable of doing exactly that, but because somehow we knew that this time, He wouldn't. Kevin eventually asked his father if he would please stop praying for that miracle. He said, "I've had my miracle—I was given eight extra years with my family."

When Kevin passed away, we received many beautiful flower and plant arrangements. I love flowers, but I've always thought that for their cost, they die way too quickly. The flowers from the funeral died before my mind had even accepted that Kevin had died. But the miracle is, one of the plants is still alive. Kevin discovered early in our marriage that I am a plant killer. His solution was to give me a cactus. I killed it, too. The only things I manage to keep alive in my home are those things that can thank me for the food I put in them. So, the fact that I have a plant that is still growing and green and alive can only mean one thing … Kevin must be taking care of it.

Perhaps the greatest miracle of all that I've witnessed is my very own "miracle wall." When Kevin was first diagnosed, we had a family discussion on miracles. I used pictures to illustrate miracles that have been documented throughout history. We discussed how grand the Old Testament miracles were—the building of an ark, or Daniel's spending the night in a lion's den unharmed. Modern-day miracles included the Mormon pioneers' crops being rescued from crickets by sea gulls and single mothers walking hundreds of miles with their children across the plains. And of course the many miracles the Savior performed—healing the lame, the blind, the sick. I wanted my children to know that miracles still exist, just as the Source of all miracles does, too. I hung these pictures on our wall upstairs with the words "We believe in miracles."

The miracle is that every single one of them is still hanging on the wall. One little piece of masking tape and they are still hanging. I can't keep Christmas cards hanging on the wall for one month, and these pictures still hang there after over a year. There is no way I can take them down now. I guess I've kind of been waiting for them to fall down so I can pick them up off the floor, stack them together, and tuck them away in a file along with the memories and experiences that prove miracles still happen. Even if it's not the miracle you really, really wanted.

Hope.

My dear friend Susie sent me a decorative letter "H" for my birthday. That "H" can represent a lot of things. Obviously, Hegewald. A name we will forever have to spell to others. On good days, I look at it as representing Happy or Home. Other days, Hardship, Heartache, or Hades. But when I look at that "H" displayed by our family portrait, I most often think of Hope. Hope has had a special place in my heart, and near my heart, throughout this challenge. My sister-in-law, Christy, gave me a necklace with the word *hope* on it. I love it and I wear it constantly. I take it off at night, but part of my brush-my-teeth morning routine includes putting my hope back on. What hope stands for changes. Somedays, I hope for comfort. Others, I hope for strength. Mostly, I hope for understanding. Not only do I wear hope near my heart, I wear it on my wrist. I continue to wear my "Hope for Hegewald" band as a reminder of the hundreds of people who rallied with us during Kevin's battle. Probably the thing I wear that symbolizes the most hope is Kevin's wedding band on my ring finger. In the final moments of closing the casket, I slipped Kevin's ring off his finger and onto my own. I actually just didn't have a pocket or purse to put it in, so I slid it beneath my own wedding ring for safekeeping. And there it has remained for the past year. It's the perfect reminder that Kevin and I belong to one another for eternity.

Lately, I have become a student of hope. I figured if I was wearing it, I'd better understand it. Bruce R. McConkie states, "Hope is the desire of faithful people to gain eternal salvation in the kingdom of God hereafter. It is not a flimsy, ethereal desire, one without assurance that the desired consummation will be received, but a desire coupled with full expectation of receiving the coveted reward." I am not going to pretend that I come close to understanding all of that, but after reading this, the "Hope for Hegewald" bands took on new meaning … What exactly had we been hoping for? While we were hoping for a miracle, did we inadvertently petition the Lord for something even greater—the "coveted reward" of eternal life?

In *The Book of Mormon*, the prophet Mormon states, "And what is it that ye shall hope for? Behold I say unto you that ye shall have hope through the atonement of Christ and the power of his resurrection, to be raised unto life eternal, and this because of your faith in him according to the promise" (Moroni 7:41). I know that Kevin is now one step closer to receiving eternal life. He was righteous, he was obedient, he was faithful, he endured to the end.

So I am going to keep wearing all of my hope. It will remind me that the greatest things to hope for are yet to come. And when my time comes to join Kevin, I hope that I will have as many friends petitioning on my behalf that I, too, am deserving of hope.

The End.

One of my most real moments during this past year occurred in the elementary school library. I dutifully report every Monday morning to help thirty-two curious second graders check out books. I can honestly say that this hour of volunteer work is the only consistent thing of the entire past year other than my sister's daily phone calls and me getting out of bed. Recently, Sam's teacher pulled me aside and asked, "You seem to be doing remarkably well …" (I appreciated the fact that she had noticed that I was out of my pajamas, with makeup on, every time I reported to duty) "… I was just wondering, are you really? Or are you just faking it?"

I wanted to tell her about the healing power of my crying chair. I wanted to tell her how I was the recipient of love from hundreds of Kevin's best friends who were showing me how much they loved him. I wanted to tell her that I believe in a world after this one, a much kinder one, where Kevin is waiting for me. I especially wanted to tell her that even though I had lost one best friend, I had found another in my Savior. But I didn't. When I opened my mouth the words just flew out, "Oh, I'm totally faking it."

How long will I have to keep faking it? Every day I am faced with the challenge of trying to find joy in a world of shattered dreams. One day I watched an old, gray-haired couple walking the aisles of Costco together. If they'd been holding hands as they shuffled along, I probably wouldn't have noticed them. But the old lady was fussing at her husband to quit taking so much time looking at everything. He just looked at her lovingly and smiled. I could barely hold back the tears. That was supposed to be Kevin and me!!

But nothing sets off a quicker panic attack than looking in the mirror. On the rare days when I don't see the old lady peering back at me, and I actually see a young forty-three-year-old, that's when the dread sets in. I stare at the looonng life I have ahead of me. And I wonder how I'm going to survive.

I do realize that that is much like wondering how you are ever going to run 26.2 miles with your foot resting on the starting line. I think it will be the milestones that will prove to me that life is still moving. Graduations, church mission calls, marriages, grandbabies. My heart swells already with the bittersweet conflict each of those moments will bring. I anticipate the sorrow I will feel, and the sorrow my children will feel, that Kevin is not there to share those moments with us. But I know that he will be. And as painful as each of those milestones will be, I will welcome each one gladly, as doing these things will show that my children have decided that life is still worth living. I especially hope they have lots and lots of babies! I can't wait to hold and squeeze and smell each one, knowing that their granddad was doing the same just moments before me. My heart will be conflicted and I will still wonder how a moment of my greatest sorrow can also be a moment of my greatest blessing. Looking in the mirror, I wonder, when that time finally comes, will my soul be filled with happiness again? I hope so. But if not, I know what to do. I am a master of it.

I will smile.

Made in the USA
Las Vegas, NV
01 March 2023